T0317686

TRADES ABOUT
TO HAPPEN

Founded in 1807, John Wiley & Sons is the oldest independent publishing company in the United States. With offices in North America, Europe, Australia, and Asia, Wiley is globally committed to developing and marketing print and electronic products and services for our customers' professional and personal knowledge and understanding.

The Wiley Trading series features books by traders who have survived the market's ever-changing temperament and have prospered—some by reinventing systems, others by getting back to basics. Whether a novice trader, professional, or somewhere in-between, these books will provide the advice and strategies needed to prosper today and well into the future.

For a list of available titles, visit our web site at www.WileyFinance.com.

TRADES ABOUT TO HAPPEN

A Modern Adaptation of the Wyckoff Method

David H. Weis

Foreword by Dr. Alexander Elder

WILEY

Cover image: © istockphoto.com/liangpv
Cover design: Wiley

Published by John Wiley & Sons, Inc., Hoboken, New Jersey.
Published simultaneously in Canada.

Charts created using TradeStation. ©TradeStation Technologies, Inc. 2001–2012. All rights reserved. No
investment or trading advice, recommendation, or opinions are being given or intended.

Charts created by MetaStock, a Thomson Reuters Company.

For general information on our other products and services or for technical support, please contact our
Customer Care Department within the United States at (800) 762-2974, outside the United States at
(317) 572-3993 or fax (317) 572-4002.

Wiley publishes in a variety of print and electronic formats and by print-on-demand. Some material
included with standard print versions of this book may not be included in e-books or in print-on-demand.
If this book refers to media such as a CD or DVD that is not included in the version you purchased,
you may download this material at http://booksupport.wiley.com. For more information about Wiley
products, visit www.wiley.com.

Library of Congress Cataloging-in-Publication Data:

Weis, David H.
   Trades about to happen : a modern adaptation of the Wyckoff method / David H. Weis.
      pages cm -- (Wiley trading series)
   Includes index.
   ISBN 978-0-470-48780-8 (cloth); 978-0-470-48780 (ebk); 978-1-118-25870-5 (ebk);
978-1-118-23362-7 (ebk)
   1. Stocks—Charts, diagrams, etc.   2. Stock price forecasting.
3. Investment analysis.   4. Wyckoff, Richard Demille, 1873-1935. I. Title.
   HG6041.W885W45 2013
   332.63'2042—dc23

                                                                2012046824

Printed in the United States of America
SKY10031667_112921

This book is dedicated to my wife, Karen,
and to the memory of my parents.

For the gods perceive things in the future;
Ordinary people things in the present;
But the wise perceive things about to happen.

—**Philostratos,** *Life of Apollonies of Tyana*

CONTENTS

A free digital file containing full-size copies of all charts shown in this book
is available from the author. Contact him at dhw@weisonwyckoff.com.

"When you go fishin' in a lake, you don't just row out to the middle and throw a line in the water. You go where the fish live—around the edges and near the sunken trees. Same way, you enter trades near the edges of congestion zones, where bulls or bears are so exhausted that a small amount of pressure can reverse a trend."

I've often heard these and other pronouncements, delivered in David's Southern drawl, in my Traders' Camps. Now it is a pleasure to see them in his book, available to you even if you can't travel to a week-long Camp and study with David in person.

David is a quiet man who spends day after day in solitude in his trading room, but he has played a large role in the development of many serious traders. When discussing markets with friends, I often hear: "This is where David would draw a line." His way of reading charts has been taken up by hundreds of his students.

Expanding on classical works of Richard Wyckoff, written almost a century ago, David has built a modern superstructure of market analysis. The changing heights of price bars, accompanied by rising or falling bars of volume are the basic irreducible elements from which David builds his market analysis. He uses these patterns to read the behavior of crowds across all markets and timeframes—and then to place his orders.

All trades leave indelible tracks on price and volume charts. David focuses on them—and these charts speak to him. Now, in this book, he teaches you to read their language.

David's sharp focus on price/volume behavior reminds me of a teacher I had in medical school. She was shy and a little deaf, and usually stood in the back during grand rounds. We knew that she was so observant and so attuned to patients' body language that when professors disagreed about a diagnosis, they'd ask for her opinion. A person who watches intently, on the basis of a great deal of experience and without any hidden agenda can see deeper than most.

A careful reading of this book will open your eyes to the huge importance of false breakouts—what David calls springs (when they point down) and upthrusts (when they point up). He promises: "once you become attuned to the behavior of a spring and upthrust your eyes will be opened to an action signal that works in all time periods. The spring can provide the impetus for a short-term pop playable by day-traders or serve as the catalyst for long-term capital gains."

Having sat for hours in the back of the room while David was lecturing and showing trade examples, false breakouts have become one of my key patterns to trade. Now you can be guided through dozens of charts by David, moving forward bar by bar, as you learn to read their messages and anticipate trend reversals.

The chapter on absorption will teach you to gauge the strength of the current trend. Is that trend moving forward like "the Greek phalanx marching in step across the Plain of Troy" as David puts it—or is its advance being absorbed by growing supply, which precedes a reversal? Now, as your eyes move across David's charts, you'll see how their price and volume patterns reveal their secret weaknesses or strengths.

Do not rush as you read this book. To fully benefit from it you need to let its many messages sink in. Be sure to apply David's concepts to current charts, watch them open up to you and become more meaningful before returning to the book and studying another dozen pages. This isn't a quickie book—it took David years to write, and the more attention you give it, the deeper will be your benefit.

Happy reading and happy trading!

Dr. Alexander Elder
www.elder.com
New York City, 2013

ACKNOWLEDGMENTS

I am totally indebted to my long-time friend, Dr. Alex Elder, who has allowed me to take part in his exotic trading camps. He has been the driving force behind the writing of this book. He has always been willing to offer support and helpful suggestions, and he opened the doors to make the publication by Wiley possible. I am also grateful to the help received from Alfred Tagher and Bob Fulks. They have been instrumental in the programming of my custom charting tools. Also, to my many students whose needs have helped me crystallize different approaches to teaching the Wyckoff material. As a former teacher, I consider their successes to be my greatest reward.

TRADES ABOUT TO HAPPEN

Introduction

Richard Wyckoff came to Wall Street in 1888. The details of his 40-year career are chronicled in his autobiography, *Wall Street Ventures and Adventures* (1930). The tales of the large operators he observed and the inside story of their manipulative campaigns make interesting reading. But his search to develop a "trained judgment" for trading offers the most compelling and inspiring story. Describing his progress as of 1905, Wyckoff wrote:

> I had now spent the greater part of seventeen years in Wall Street—as a boy, clerk, silent partner and managing partner in Stock Exchange houses. But with all I had seen, studied, and observed, I had yet no well-defined plan or method for money-making in the stock market, either for my clients or for myself.[1]

Up to this point in his career, two threads wind through his experiences. First, big traders spend hours studying stock transactions as they appear on the ticker tape. Second, he saw the need for a college or educational service to teach the "inner workings of the stock market." He wanted to show how the public was repeatedly bilked by the large manipulators in the market. In late 1907, as Wall Street suffered from the aftershock of another panic, Wyckoff decided to write an educational publication—a monthly magazine called *The Ticker*—consisting of articles about the stock market. The bulk of the writing rested on Wyckoff's shoulders, and the pressure to

[1] Richard D. Wyckoff, *Wall Street Ventures and Adventures* (New York: Greenwood Press, 1968), 134.

find new material led him into many facets of the stock, bond, and commodity markets. He tested mechanical trading methods based on statistics and numerous theories presented to him by readers. While he ultimately moved in a different direction, he realized that charts provided a better record of price history than pure statistics. As his study of charts and stock market techniques progressed, he turned to the ticker tape. "I saw more and more that the action of stocks reflected the plans and purposes of those who dominated them. I began to see possibilities of judging from the very tape what these master minds were doing."[2] Under the guidance of a former floor trader at the stock exchange, Wyckoff began a serious study of tape reading. His observations became the impetus for a series of tape reading articles in *The Ticker* and his readers clamored for more. This original series of articles provided the material for Wyckoff's first book, *Studies in Tape Reading*, published in 1910 under the pseudonym Rollo Tape. About this book, Wyckoff later wrote in his autobiography:

> The purpose of the self-training and the continued application of the methods suggested in *Studies in Tape Reading* was to develop an intuitive judgment, which would be the natural outcome of spending twenty-seven hours a week at the ticker over many months and years.[3]

In the next few years, the price swings in stocks became larger, and Wyckoff applied his tape reading methods to the broader movements of the market. The public demanded more frequent trading recommendations with less emphasis on the analysis. This spawned his *Trend Letter*, a weekly one-page sheet containing a list of trades. It grew in popularity until its following became too large and unwieldy causing Wyckoff to seek privacy. He ended the publication in 1917 after achieving the largest following of any individual on Wall Street since the 1890s.

Wyckoff did not drift into obscurity. He wrote several more books. *The Ticker* was transformed into the *Magazine of Wall Street,* with which he was heavily involved until declining health forced his retirement in 1926. In the final years of his life, Wyckoff returned to the idea of educating the public and conceived a Wall Street College. His health dictated a less monumental effort. In 1932, he turned his attention to a course explaining his method of trading in stocks. The original course was divided into two divisions: Division One, *A*

---

[2] Ibid., 168.

[3] Ibid., 176.

Course of Instruction in Stock Market Science and Technique; and Division Two, *A Course of Instruction in Tape Reading and Active Trading.* Wyckoff died in 1934.

Since 1934, the "Wyckoff course," as it is known, has preserved Wyckoff's place in the pantheon of market masters. Thousands of traders and investors have taken the course, which is still offered today by the Stock Market Institute in Phoenix, Arizona. Over the past 80 years, the course has been modified and updated to accommodate changes in market conditions without disturbing Wyckoff's original work. It contains the specific details of Wyckoff's trading/analytical methods. His chapter on "Determining the Trend of the Market by the Vertical Bar Chart of the NY Times Average of 50 Stocks" captures the essence of his work and provides the guiding light for my book.

Many students who take the Wyckoff course today focus on the models of accumulation and distribution. Wyckoff never devised such an interpretation of accumulation and distribution. They were added after his death. He certainly discussed some of the features of market behavior that were incorporated into these models. Accumulation and distribution are taught today as behavior revealed on bar charts with volume. Yet, when Wyckoff mentioned these terms, it was mostly in regard to point-and-figure charts and never with specific components. It is my opinion that these models were created by his former associates to add specificity to the course. As expressed in his autobiography, Wyckoff wanted to teach students how to develop a trader's feel— intuition. Specificity sells better than intuition; it's more tangible. I believe there is too much dependency on recognizing patterns of behavior rather than on the art of reading bar charts. These patterns can quickly become cookie prints, like geometric formations, into which price movement is stuffed by those looking for a quick, no-think fix. They lead to rigid rather than creative thinking. They often frustrate the new student of Wyckoff analysis who might not realize the world of chart reading is gray, not black or white. One has to have an open mind rather than being fixed on a preconceived ideal. While the metaphors created by Bob Evans, a famous teacher of the Wyckoff course, describing springs, up-thrusts, ice lines, and so on, are colorful and instructive, Wyckoff never used such terminology; however, that does not make them forbidden or useless. On the contrary, they are very helpful. Wyckoff was first and foremost a tape reader. As the markets grew more robust and volatile, he applied his tape reading skills to bar chart reading, where emphasis is placed on price range, position of the close, and volume. Wyckoff obviously knew the importance of trend lines, channels, and support/resistance lines; however, they are given greater coverage in the modern course.

I have borrowed from Wyckoff's original writings as well as the concepts of Bob Evans. My approach, which incorporates price range, close, and volume, also utilizes what I call "the story of the lines," that is, the story of the price/volume behavior as framed and interconnected by lines drawn on charts. The lines bring the price movement into focus and guide one toward the behavior that prompts action in the market. Thus, I am trying to find trades on charts rather than figuring out if accumulation or distribution is taking place. A real gold mine of information lies in Wyckoff's method of reading bar charts. It has become a lost art.

The purpose of my book is to show how one can logically interpret bar charts and wave charts to find trades about to happen. By studying the chart examples in this book, I believe the reader will gain tremendous insight into reading what markets say about themselves. It may seem tedious at first, but, through practice and repetition (repetition is the mother of wisdom!), it will become second nature. It will give you the ability to locate turning points of different degrees.

In the studies that appear throughout this book, we will:

- Compare effort of the buying or selling with the reward (i.e., volume versus upward or downward progress).

- Watch for ease of movement or lack of movement (i.e., wide price bars versus narrow price bars).

- Consider the meaning of the close within the range of a price bar.

- Watch for shortening of upward or downward thrust.

- Watch for follow-through or lack of follow-through after penetrations of support/resistance (this includes the notion of springs and upthrusts).

- Watch for tests of high-volume or "vertical" areas where price accelerated upward or downward.

- Consider the interaction of price with trend lines, channels, and support/resistance lines, which often highlight the price/volume story.

In the second half of this book, I will introduce adaptations I have made to Wyckoff's original tape-reading tools, which are better suited for the enormous volatility of today's stock and futures markets. These can be applied to intraday and daily price movement, and software has been created for use in real time. To find trades on any type of chart, we will be guided by the following statement, made long ago by Richard Wyckoff:

> Successful tape reading [chart reading] is a study of Force. It requires ability to judge which side has the greatest pulling power and one must have the courage to go with that side. There are critical points which occur in each swing just as in the life of a business or of an individual. At these junctures it seems as though a feather's weight on either side would determine the immediate trend. Any one who can spot these points has much to win and little to lose.[4]

After reading this book, I guarantee you will never go back to the previous way you viewed charts. I have no secrets and will teach all I know about Wyckoff and price/volume behavior. Confucius said: "A true teacher is one who knows (and makes known) the New, by revitalizing the Old."

---

[4] Rollo Tape [pseud.], *Studies in Tape Reading* (Burlington, VT: Fraser, 1910), 95.

CHAPTER 1

Where to Find Trades

An Overview

Finding trades is like finding fish. Fish can be randomly caught in any part of a lake, but they tend to congregate in specific areas at different times of the year. Similarly, big trades can be hooked at any point on a chart, but they appear with greater frequency around the edges of trading ranges.

Trading ranges do not have set patterns. Prices may twist and turn in a myriad of ways before a trading range is resolved. In general, however, trading ranges are rectangular shaped with prices swinging back and forth between the upper and lower boundaries or coiling into apexes. But we are concerned with the dynamics of trading ranges rather than any geometrical shape. When trading ranges evolve over many months or years, they often expand their boundaries and contain numerous smaller ranges. The boundaries of trading ranges are repeatedly tested and/or penetrated as the buyers and sellers struggle for dominance. Whenever the boundaries are breached, follow-through or the lack of follow-through becomes the deciding factor. After breakouts or breakdowns occur, prices often retest these areas.

In the next few chapters, we will examine the characteristics of price/volume behavior at these various points. Keep in mind we are dealing with trading ranges of all sizes and not solely at tops or bottoms. The behavior described here occurs on all charts regardless of their time period. With practice, one can readily identify the behavior areas circled on Figure 1.1.

The first step involves drawing the trading ranges—a seemingly easy task that requires an eye for horizontal relationships.

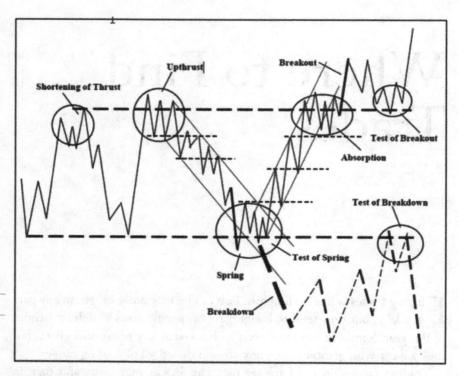

FIGURE 1.1 Where to Find Trades Diagram

Look at the six trading ranges (TR1–TR6) on Figure 1.2 of Nasdaq futures. By repeatedly framing the support and resistance lines, we see how trends consist of individual ranges and the turning points emerge from the otherwise tangle of price movement. These turning points—springs, upthrusts, absorption, and tests of breakout/breakdowns—serve as action signals.

In later chapters, volume will be incorporated into the understanding of this price behavior. But, first, we will focus on the lines. Reading a chart without lines is like studying a world map without boundary lines. It's the subject of the next two chapters and serves as the first step in my method for reading charts.

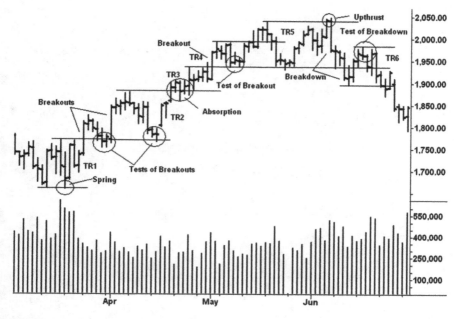

FIGURE 1.2 Nasdaq Continuation Daily Chart
Source: TradeStation.

Drawing Lines

So much of trading and technical analysis looks easy. On the Internet, for example, you can find all sorts of trading systems showing how trades were initiated at point A and sold at point B for a 3,000 percent profit in only four months. A book on technical analysis might glorify buying breakouts or the breaking of a trend line. Trends do require breakouts in order to persist but, unfortunately, many fail. The penetration of a trend line per se guarantees little. What preceded the trend line break and the way it occurred reveals more. Then we have the skeptics who fall back on the old saying, "Lines are drawn to be broken." So what! Price movement evolves and we redraw.

Drawing support and resistance lines might seem the subject of Charting 101. Some say it's for beginners. But you would be surprised by how many people cannot tailor the placement of their lines to highlight the behavior within a trading range. Even fewer have learned to recognize horizontal lines around which prices have revolved. Let's first look at a typical trading range and imagine we are examining Figure 2.1 of Level 3 Communications from the viewpoint of the right-most day (December 26, 2003). We see a great deal of lateral movement after the September 25 high. A resistance line is drawn across this high, and the initial low on October 2 serves as the support line. Why did I choose these two points for resistance and support levels? The high and low on October 15 and 24 could have worked equally well—maybe even better as the top occurred on October 15. In real time, I might have framed the trading range with the October high-low. But looking in retrospect from right to left, the two bold lines tell a better story. They dramatize the failures in October and November to move upward or lower.

At two of these points, the sellers attempted to take control of the stock and drive prices lower. Each time, however, the buyers checked the decline and prices recovered. This is important information. It tells us the buyers remain dominant. The support line brings the struggle between the buyers and sellers into focus. During the latter half of December, notice the lifting of supports as the buyers gradually overcame the selling pressure. Such a sustained rise in price with most of the closes near the daily highs tells a more bullish story than wide flailing action. It indicates the stock is in strong hands.

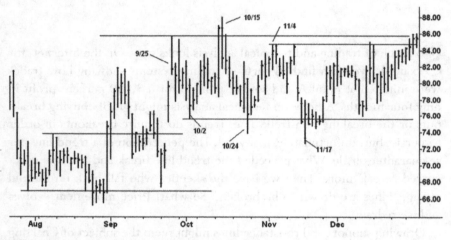

FIGURE 2.1 Level 3 Communications (LVLT) Daily Chart
Source: TradeStation.

The resistance line drawn across the September 25 high was penetrated on October 14, where prices registered their highest close. At this point, the buyers were seemingly in control. On the following day, however, the sellers turned back the advance and drove prices back down into the trading range. This reversal action threatened the uptrend from the August low until prices refused to break down on October 24 and November 17. Notice the October high has not played any role during this trading range. A line of resistance did form across the November 4 high as it blocked the two rallies in December. It marked the high of a trading range that began from the October 24 low. It is not uncommon to see trading ranges within larger ranges—especially when they span several months.

Since the trading range in LVLT spanned about 20 percent of the October peak price, we have to consider it of intermediate size. On hourly charts, we find many small trading ranges that swing less than 1 percent from high to low. These may last only a few days at most. While the support/resistance lines may not always tell as vivid a story about failed opportunities as we saw in LVLT, they do show (in the case of a downtrend) the steady progression of lower lows and highs.

As demonstrated on the Agnico Eagle Mines hourly (Figure 2.2), the lines reveal how prices interact with previously drawn lines. Trading range AA' dominates the chart. It contains a smaller range, BC, which fails to support the market. The breakdown to support line D leads to one last rally into the larger trading range. This rally ends with an upward spike on January 17, 2012. The weak close on this price bar revealed the presence of selling. Support line D also serves as an axis line as prices repeatedly tried to recover from below it. The last of these occurred on the up-move from support line E. By drawing these lines, the trader can anticipate price swings to peak or bottom around previous support/resistance lines. They become an important part of a trader's arsenal—especially when combined with trend lines, channels, and price/volume behavior.

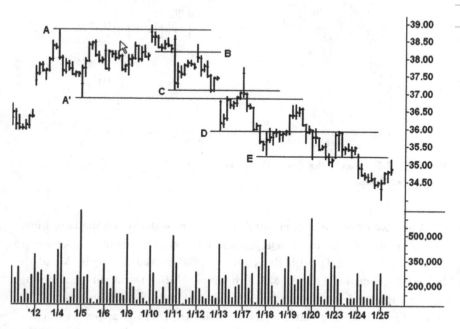

FIGURE 2.2 Agnico Eagle Mines Hourly Chart
Source: TradeStation.

Some of the most useful axis lines appear on daily charts. On the March 2006 bond daily chart (Figure 2.3), resistance line A, drawn across the late November 2005 high, provided support in January 2006 and resistance twice in February 2006. The two rallies in February were tests of the breakdown below line A. The axis line alone does not reveal strength or weakness; nor does it signal to buy or sell. It simply shows a level that has repeatedly served as support and resistance. Prices may have revolved around it for several weeks or months. Many times the final rally in a top formation or the final downswing in a bottom will occur along an axis line. What makes this line most meaningful is the price/volume behavior around it. But one first must learn to see the lines. With practice, you will be able to see all of the linear relationships at a glance.

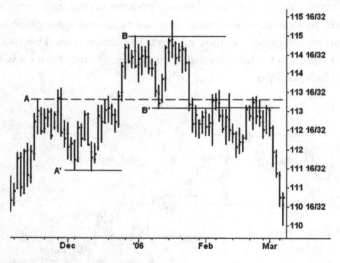

FIGURE 2.3   March 2006 Bonds Daily Chart
Source: TradeStation.

When we draw these horizontal lines, we repeatedly see the false moves on either side of a trading range. Compare the false breakout on October 15 in LVLT (Figure 2.1) with the January spike in March bonds. All of this behavior stands out with the aid of the lines. Notice the small trading range in LVLT during July–August 2003. It, like the sell-off on November 17, led to a bullish turnaround after a false breakdown. Trading ranges are horizontal patterns. They are resolved in three ways: a long, drawn-out period of lateral movement that tires out the most diehard longs; by the formation of an apex in which the amplitude of the price swings narrows to a point of equilibrium; or a false breakout/breakdown. In the chapters ahead, we will explain much more of this behavior.

Trend lines depict the angle of advance or decline. They are dynamic support and resistance lines as opposed to the static horizontal lines that frame trading ranges. In a downtrend, a trend line is drawn across successively lower highs. It seems uncanny that a trend line can be drawn across highs, for example, in January and March, which later provides resistance in July and September. The resistance points in July and September are known as touch points—that is, places within a trend where rallies halted against the trend line. Touch points add validity to a trend line. In an uptrend, a trend line is drawn across the rising supports. It is called the demand line as it marks the point where buying repeatedly emerges. Similarly, the downtrend line across highs is called the supply line. As will be discussed, these are combined to create trend channels.

Let's begin with some samples of uptrend lines. Normally, they are drawn from the low point of a decline. We do not want to draw a trend line through price movement to reach the second anchor point. On the daily continuation chart of the 10-year Treasury note (Figure 2.4) we see the simplest uptrend line. The lows of November 4 and December 5 serve as the anchor points. This line provided support on three additional corrections. Although

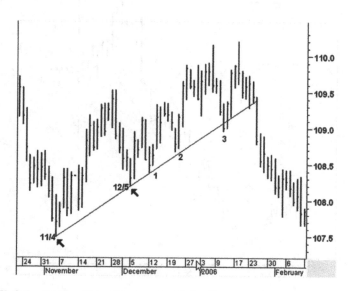

FIGURE 2.4 10-Year Note Continuation Daily Chart
Source: MetaStock.

prices broke slightly below the line at point 3, they quickly recovered to make a new high. You can immediately see the inherent risks in automatically going short solely on the penetration of an uptrend line. As previously stated, the behavior prior to the trend line break and the way it occurs tell the story. After you finish reading this book, the bearish behavior prior to the January 25 breakdown will be apparent. Two months later the 10-year fell below 10524.

Trend lines are drawn from the perspective of the last day on the chart. One looks across the chart like a surveyor staking out land for development. A second daily LVLT chart (Figure 2.5) is shown through December 1, 2005. Looking backward, we fit a minor trend line onto the rally from the October low. We do not use the precise low as the first anchor point. If we did, the line would not fit the angle of advance. Instead, we draw the line from the low of the fourth day (point 1). If a steep uptrend line ("a") is drawn from this low, it will pass through price movement. The low at point 2 is a better second anchor for the line is free and clear of other prices and it later provides support at point 3. One more factor: at point 2, we do not know prices will continue upward. Connecting points 1 and 2 creates a

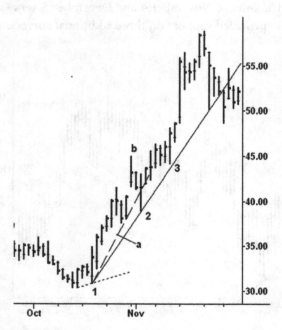

FIGURE 2.5 LVLT Daily Chart
Source: TradeStation.

tentative line until the high at "b" is exceeded. A rally above "b" constitutes an uptrend. I am not so terribly rigid, for the line can always be redrawn later. If one applied the same reasoning to the 10-year chart (Figure 2.4), the uptrend line would not be confirmed until the rally in late December exceeded the November high. Because the December touch points at 1 and 2 hold along the line, I would not hesitate to draw it.

If LVLT (Figure 2.5) had immediately rallied above 58.95 after December 1, the trend line shown here would no longer depict the angle of advance. A new line drawn from point 1 would not capture the angle of advance. This also occurs after lengthy periods of lateral movement within a larger uptrend. The monthly chart (Figure 2.6) of the Dow from the March 2003 low provides a good example. Here, we have an uptrend line drawn across the 2003 and 2004 lows. But the correction from the March 2005 high penetrates this line, and six months of lateral movement follow. When the trend resumes, we could redraw the trend line off the 2003 and October 2005 lows, but it would be too shallow. A better choice involves drawing a second parallel line and anchoring it off the 2005 low. This maintains the original angle of advance, but it did not do a good job of pinpointing the October 2007 high.

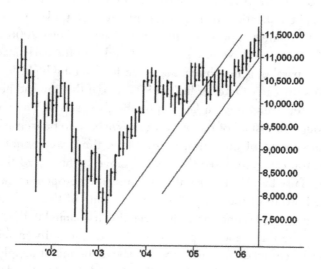

FIGURE 2.6 Dow Jones Industrial Average Monthly Chart
Source: TradeStation.

Reference to parallel lines brings us to the subject of trend channels. In an up-channel, the demand line is drawn across lows and a parallel supply line is drawn across an intervening high. Figure 2.7 describes the anchor points and the order in which they are connected.

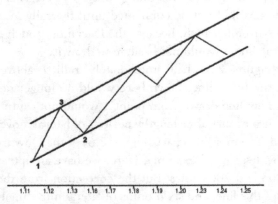

FIGURE 2.7 Normal Up-Channel Diagram

You can quickly see this pattern by drawing a line across the high of point "b" on the LVLT chart (Figure 2.5). The ideal up-channel will have several additional touch points. It should capture most of the price work within its boundaries. A rally above the top of an up-channel is often a better overbought indication than most mathematical tools. A more interesting set of channels appears on the daily chart of April 2006 live cattle (Figure 2.8). Here we have low points at 1 and 2 in the early stages of the advance. The parallel is not drawn across an intervening high. Instead, it is drawn across the early October high at 90 cents. If the line had been drawn across the intervening high in late September, the supply line would have passed through almost all of the price work. We have to be free and creative with the placement of our lines. At the same time, we cannot force the placement. You can readily see the trading range at the top of the chart. It consists of a false breakout above the high and a wide-open break that penetrated the bottom of the range. These were some of the clues that prices were turning down. I cannot omit the steep down-channel to the April 2006 low. You see the three anchor points and the anemic rally in mid-March. Notice how prices made upward progress above the minor supply line during this small lateral movement. In April, prices plunged to the demand line and reversed upward. This is the largest rally within the down-move. I hope you see the license taken with the anchor points used in this down-channel. Perhaps in real time I would have begun differently, but once the contract broke below 90 cents, the best channel would have become apparent.

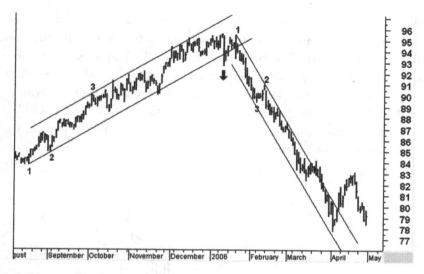

FIGURE 2.8 April 2006 Live Cattle Daily Chart
Source: MetaStock.

Something else has to be mentioned regarding up-channels. Bob Evans, one of the most prominent and enthusiastic teachers of the Wyckoff course, used to prepare cassette tapes on which he discussed aspects of chart reading. He devised colorful metaphors for describing different kinds of market behavior. In one of his most famous tapes, he shared with his listeners a learning tool devised by a former student. It was called "The Shell Diver's Tragedy" and dealt with the behavior after the breakdown below the demand line of an up-channel. He compared the market's rise within the channel to a diver who picks shells off the ocean floor and returns to the surface (i.e., supply line) where he places them in a floating basket. At some point during this activity, he falls below his usual depth (demand line) and develops a cramp. He tries valiantly to reach the surface but falls short and rolls over for the final time. On the cattle chart, point 1 marks the final attempt to reach the top of the up-channel. From this tale, we learn to watch the character of the rally following the break of the demand line. If prices recover and surge to new highs, the odds favor a resumption of the uptrend.

On the monthly chart of the Commodity Research Bureau (CRB) Index (Figure 2.9), we see the "noninflationary" rise from the 2001 low. This steep advance fits beautifully within the up-channel originally drawn from points 1, 2, and 3. Notice the numerous touch points at later dates.

After the low in January 2005, when energy prices began to rise exponentially, the advance steepened and prices trended along the supply line. A second parallel line is drawn from the high at point 4 and it stops the next two up-moves. As illustrated on the monthly Dow chart (Figure 2.6), a second parallel line broadens a channel and provides a useful guide for viewing price movement. In the case of the CRB Index, the lines do not indicate the uptrend has ended. It steepened and continued for several more years.

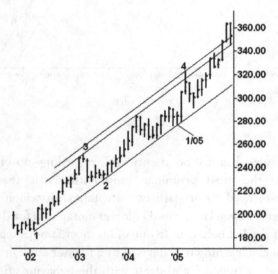

FIGURE 2.9 CRB Index Monthly Chart
Source: TradeStation.

One more type of line deserves attention. It is the reverse trend line and reverse trend channel. The basic look is sketched in Figure 2.10. They are normally drawn with dashed lines to set them apart from normal trend lines/channels. Some uptrends will not fit in the normal channels we have previously discussed. Because of their steepness, they require drawing a reverse trend line across rising highs—points 1 and 2. To make a reverse up-channel, a parallel line is drawn across an intervening low. In the diagram (Figure 2.10), price does not interact with the lower line of the up-channel; however, in the future, it could provide support. Many times, a normal uptrend line will combine nicely with a reverse trend line to form converging lines. Some technicians refer to this as a rising wedge. In the instance of an uptrend, the converging lines often indicate a rally is tiring or losing momentum. When prices are falling within a pattern of converging lines, it usually signifies the decline is nearing a low.

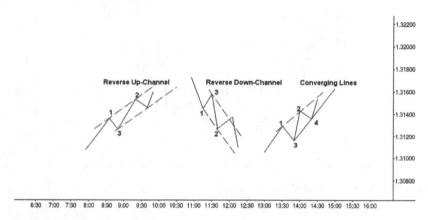

FIGURE 2.10 Reverse Trend Channel Diagrams
Source: TradeStation.

Figure 2.11 presents an unnamed chart with the three types of reverse trend lines/channels mentioned above. The decline on the left side of the chart fits into a reverse down-channel (AA). It is drawn by connecting the two lows, and then the parallel is attached to the intervening high. The reverse up-channel CC' is much steeper and price moves above line C. Notice the sell-off from this high found support on parallel line C'. A move above or below a reverse trend line often will mark the end of a swing. I know an ingenious trader who has developed software showing how many stocks per day have reached or exceeded reverse trend lines. In an uptrend, a large increase in the number of these often indicates the market is vulnerable to a downturn. Lines BB' do not form a reverse channel. Line B is a reverse trend line that, when combined with normal trend line B', forms the converging or wedge pattern. I have never considered chart patterns of any significance except for this one, as it is most associated with ending action.

I cannot stress enough how often a move above or below a reverse trend line/channel will lead to a trend reversal. The Standard & Poor's (S&P) daily continuation chart (Figure 2.12) shows the price movement after the

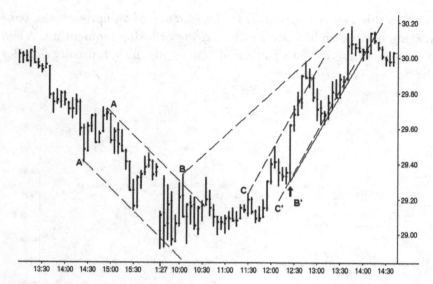

FIGURE 2.11 Reverse Channel Examples

August 2011 low. The volatile trading range AB was resolved by a thrust to new lows and an upward reversal. Notice this reversal occurred after the break below the reverse trend line within the declining wedge. Circles are drawn around the overshoot at the October 4 low and the October 27 high. The latter was above the reverse trend channel and resulted in

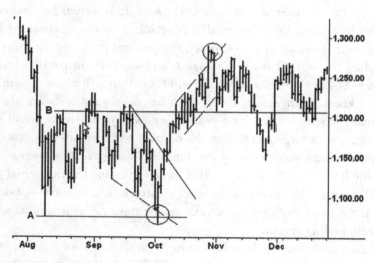

FIGURE 2.12 S&P Continuation Daily Chart
Source: TradeStation.

a 142-point sell-off. Line B served as both resistance and support during the months shown here. This line was the launch pad for a large up-move from the December low.

The live cattle quarterly chart (Figure 2.13) shows a reverse trend channel spanning many years. Looking backward from the 2011 high, one can detect the reverse trend line (A) drawn across the 1993–2003 highs. The vertical price rise in 2011 pushed prices above this line. The parallel (A') to this reverse trend line is drawn across the 1996 low. In this situation, the line passes through some of the price movement, but it was a parallel rather than a starting line. You see how frequently the market respected the parallel line. Yet it could not have been drawn until after the 2003 high. A normal up-channel is drawn across the 2002–2009 lows (B) with a parallel across the 2003 high (B'). Price rallied to the very top of this channel where we have a confluence of lines. Together, they underscore the magnitude of the potential extremity.

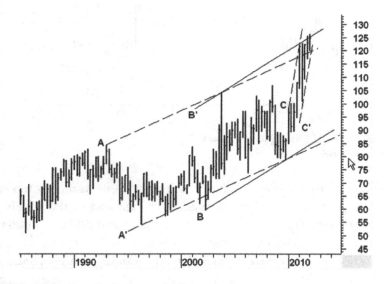

FIGURE 2.13 Live Cattle Quarterly Chart
Source: MetaStock.

The stock market reached a major high in October 2007, and most issues declined accordingly. One exception was U.S. Steel (Figure 2.14), which consolidated throughout 2007. It erupted in April 2008 and gained almost $70 per share in the next two months. The up-move exceeded the confines of any normal up-channel. After the stock rallied above the reverse trend line in June 2008, the bullish trend finally came to an end and prices collapsed. As you can see, exceeding up and down reverse trend lines must put one on alert for a trend reversal. No other trend line break has such predictive value.

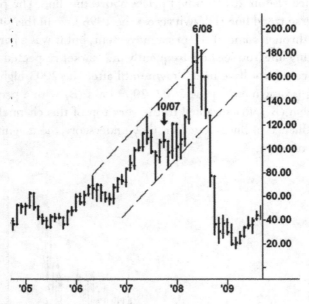

FIGURE 2.14 U.S Steel Monthly Chart
Source: TradeStation.

Some price trends defy channels. Their advance or decline is too steep to fit into a normal or broadened channel. The uptrend on the weekly July 2006 sugar chart (Figure 2.15) between May 2005 and February 2006 typifies the problem. Take a look at the five points labeled on the weekly chart. The only lines I can conceive begin with points 3 and 5. A parallel line across point 4 fails to hold as prices soar beyond its boundary. If one draws a second parallel line across point 2, the broadened channel does contain most of the price movement until the final high. This may not be a totally "legal" way to draw a channel because the high of the second parallel occurred prior to points 3 and 5. But it works. Drawing support/resistance lines, trend lines, and channels (normal, reverse, or broadened) demands open-mindedness. One must always consider other possibilities. Enough mechanics; now we are ready for the story of the lines.

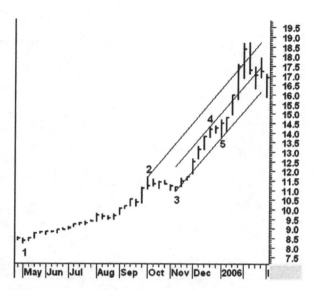

FIGURE 2.15 July 06 Sugar Weekly Chart
Source: MetaStock.

CHAPTER 3

The Story of the Lines

I cannot stress enough the importance of drawing lines all over your charts. They tell a story and make the price/volume behavior stand out. They define the angle of advance or decline within a price trend, alert one to when a market has reached an overbought or oversold point within a trend, frame trading ranges, depict prices coiling to a point of equilibrium (apex), and help forecast where to expect support or resistance on corrections. We will begin with a study of soybean oil. Figure 3.1 shows the price movement on the daily continuation chart of soybean oil between December 2001 and May 6, 2002. Let's assume today is May 6 and we are beginning to examine the behavior on this chart. I first begin with the support and resistance lines. Support line A is drawn across the January 28 low. Resistance line B is drawn across the February 5 high and resistance line C across the March 15 high. By extending these horizontal lines across the chart, we see how later corrections in March and May found support along line B. When a line alternately serves as support and resistance, I refer to it as an *axis line*. Prices tend to revolve around these axis lines. In their monumental work, *Technical Analysis of Stock Trends*, Edwards and Magee provided one of the most extensive discussions of support and resistance lines. While they never mentioned axis lines in the context described above, they duly noted the phenomenon of horizontal lines alternating as both support and resistance:

> But here is the interesting and the important fact which, curiously enough, many casual chart observers appear never to grasp: these

critical price levels constantly switch their roles from support to resistance and from resistance to support. A former top, once it has been surpassed, becomes a bottom zone in a subsequent down trend; and an old bottom, once it has been penetrated, becomes a top in a later advancing phase.[1]

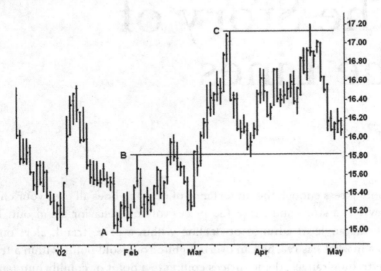

FIGURE 3.1 Soybean Oil Continuation Daily Chart
Source: TradeStation.

The support/resistance lines also frame the two trading ranges on this portion of the chart. By drawing the lines, we can better observe the attempts of either side to break out, as took place during the trench warfare of WWI. The numerous false breakouts on either side of a trading range are important tests of the opposing forces' strength. As will be discussed later, many low-risk trading opportunities are provided by these tests.

Only one important trend line can be drawn at this stage of the market's development. In Figure 3.2; trend line T is drawn across the January–February lows. Notice how prices interacted with this line in early May. Parallel line T' is drawn across the March high. This is a normal up-channel where a support line (or demand line) is drawn across two lows and a parallel resistance line (or supply line) is drawn across an intervening high.

---

[1] Robert Edwards and John Magee, *Technical Analysis of Stock Trends* (Boston: John Magee, 1987), 212.

In this case, the intervening high would be in late February. Given the subsequent price movement, a line across the actual intervening high would be meaningless. Therefore, it is drawn across a higher point on the chart. The angle of advance depicted by up-channel TT' is not steep and will not contain a larger rally. Two minor up-channels are shown within TT'. The first of these, from late February to March 15, is a normal channel. The slower price rise from the March low to the April high is also framed by a normal up-channel.

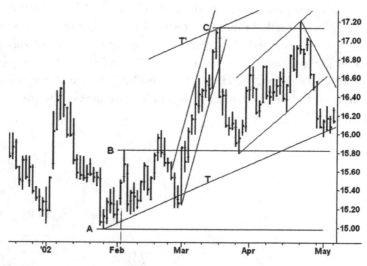

FIGURE 3.2   Soybean Oil Daily Chart 2
Source: TradeStation.

   Notice how the market rose above the top of this up-channel in April and also above resistance line C without following through. The rise above the supply line of the channel created an overbought condition that is more reliable than those provided by mathematical indicators. Without getting too far ahead of ourselves, the position of the close on the top day indicated the market had met supply (selling). The downswing from the April high is too steep for drawing channels so a simple downtrend line is drawn. At certain points in the struggle between buyers and sellers, prices often arrive at a nexus or confluence of lines. Many times, these areas produce important turning points. At the April high, we see the supply line of a minor up-channel meeting resistance line C. At the May low, we have trend line T, resistance line B, and a minor downtrend line coming together. When there is such a confluence of lines, one should be alert to the possibility of a turning point. I rarely establish a trade based on the evidence of trend lines alone. As will be discussed later, other factors are taken into account; however, if one wanted to make trades based on only one type of technical phenomenon, the lines would serve as an excellent guide.

Figure 3.3 shows the price movement through the second week of July 2002. We immediately see that the advance from the May low started with a fast, four-day rise and then slowed into an orderly stair-step affair. Several channels could have been drawn off different turning points from the May low, but by May 30 (five days from the high) channel VV' provided the best fit. This rally far exceeded the top of channel TT'. From the June 6 high, a new trading range formed. Notice how the lower boundary of this range approached former resistance line C. After the market rallied above May high, l would have drawn the channel labeled XX'. It is drawn by connecting the May–July lows and placing a parallel line across the intervening high in June.

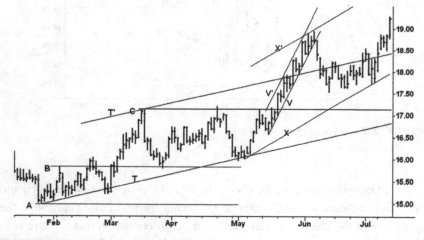

FIGURE 3.3   Soybean Oil Daily Chart 3
Source: TradeStation.

Before we leave the study of this market, one last picture is provided in Figure 3.4. Here, we see how the rally from the July low moved slightly above channel XX' creating an overbought condition. Resistance line E is drawn across the July high. From this high, the market declines until it finds support along line D. After prices surge again, trend line Y is drawn. It and line X' form a rising wedge. While I am not interested in looking for geometric patterns, the converging lines clearly show the shortening of the upward thrust. Notice how prices keep pushing through the supply line of channel XX' but fail to start a steeper angle of advance. After the sell-off from the last high above the channel, I drew resistance line F. The sell-off found support around line Y, and the market actually made a fractional new high above line F before reversing downward. At this juncture, notice the confluence of lines: resistance line F, supply line X', and support line Y all converge at this point. Support line G is drawn across the low between the final two highs, and it plays an important role over the next few weeks.

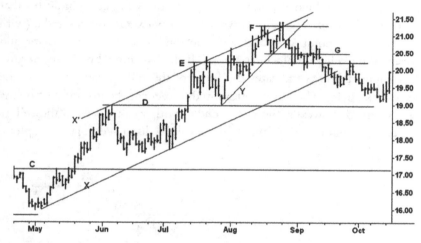

FIGURE 3.4   Soybean Oil Daily Chart 4
Source: TradeStation.

So far we have dealt only with the lines on the chart as the price movement unfolded. In Figure 3.5, eight of the most important points on the soybean oil chart are numbered for discussion. At these points, we discern ending action or clues about impending ending action. Point 1 is a false breakout above line C. Here, the market rallied above resistance but closed below the line and near the day's low. Two days later, the narrow range indicated demand was tired and price would pull back. The ensuing sell-off held on top of line B. Notice the narrowing of the price range on the low day of the sell-off. Here, the sellers seemingly had the upper hand. At point 2, however, prices reversed upward, closing above the previous day's high and putting the market in a strong position. This reversal propelled prices higher until the rally tired in early June. Note the narrow range and weak close at the June high. After a pullback and consolidation, the market returned to the upper end of the new trading range. It marked time for three days in a tight range before accelerating upward over the next two sessions. Point 3 refers to the absorption within the tight range prior to the breakout. At point 4, price rallies above the up-channel from the May low and the position of the close indicated selling was present. The pullback to point 5 tested the area where prices rose vertically. The position of the close at point 5 reflected the presence of buying. At points 6 and 7, we see how prices are struggling to continue higher. A reverse trend line (dashed) could have been drawn across the high of points 4 and 6 to highlight the market's lack of upward progress. The fractional new high at point 8 along with the weak close indicates that demand is exhausted. The cumulative behavior between points 4 and 8 (with the exception of point 5) indicates the uptrend in soybean oil is tiring and increases the likelihood of a correction. The high-volume break (see arrow) below support line G indicates the force of the selling had overcome the force of the buying. The buyers attempted to recover the ground lost below support line G; however, the rallies ended with weak closes as the sellers thwarted both efforts. All of these points will be discussed in later chapters.

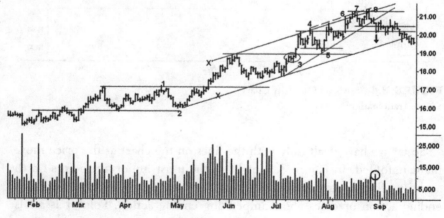

FIGURE 3.5 Soybean Oil Daily Chart 5
Source: TradeStation.

The kind of lines we have drawn on the daily soybean oil charts can be applied to longer-term charts as well. They help focus one's attention on the larger battle lines, which, in some cases, have provided support and resistance for years or decades. An awareness of a market's position within its historical framework fits the needs of the stock investor as well as those of a position trader or commercial operating in the futures markets. The long-term support/resistance lines, trend lines, and channels in conjunction with the range of the price bars (weekly, monthly, yearly) and the position of their closes can be interpreted in the same manner, as illustrated in the preceding discussion. With the study of the long-term charts, time marks the only difference. Price movement on an hourly or daily chart can be interpreted much more quickly than with monthly or yearly charts. Yet the biggest rewards come from recognizing when long-term opportunities are developing. From this information, we can then zero in on the daily chart.

Soybean oil in 2002 was such an opportunity. Figure 3.6 shows yearly cash soybean oil prices from 1931 to 2003. It tells the story of many commodities over the past 75 years:

- Prices bottomed in the early 1930s at the depth of the Depression.

- Prices rose into the high of the late 1940s under the stimulus of the Marshall Plan.

- Prices entered a period of extreme dullness until awakening in the late 1960s.

- Prices rose sharply during the mid-1970s under inflationary pressure.

- Prices entered extremely volatile trading range until bottoming in the 1999–2002 period.

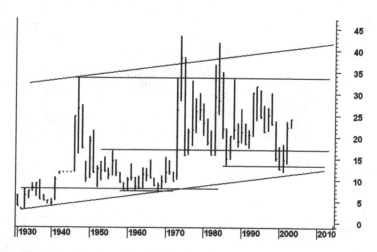

FIGURE 3.6 Cash Soybean Bean Oil Yearly Chart
Source: MetaStock.

This has been the general price pattern of many agricultural commodities produced in the United States. Horizontal resistance lines are drawn across the 1935, 1947, and 1956 highs. Look at the market's interaction with these lines. Between 1952 and 1972 soybean oil stabilized on top of the 1935 high. The 1956 high was blown away by the meteoric rise in 1973, thanks in part to export demand. This explosive rally carried through the 1947 peak, but the gains were short lived as prices promptly reversed back to the area of the 1956 high. A new trading range developed roughly on top of this previous resistance level. After 1985, prices coiled for 13 years into an apex. The breakdown from 1998 to 2000 was a terminal shakeout of the larger trading range from the 1975 low. In 2001, shortly before our study of the daily chart began, prices reversed above the 2000 high and closed near midrange. This put soybean oil on the springboard for a much larger up-move. An understanding of the market's position on the long-term chart at the beginning of 2002 gave greater meaning to the turning points in May and July. By early 2004, prices had rallied into the 34-cent area. Prices doubled again on the rise to the 2008 high (71 cents).

In Figure 3.7, we see the history of cash cocoa prices back to 1930. The major turning points in cocoa line up with those in soybean oil: low in early 1930s, top in 1947, long trading range to the low of the 1960s, huge upwave during the 1970s, and a bottom at the end of the twentieth century. In 1977, cocoa peaked at a price 74 times greater than its 1933 low. The

FIGURE 3.7 Cash Cocoa Yearly Chart
Source: MetaStock.

price range in 1977 equals the distance from 1933 to 1973. Only a semilog scale would allow one to see the earlier price history. The up-channel drawn across the 1940–1965 lows has contained almost all of the price work. In 1977, however, prices exceeded the channel. In the following year, all the gains of 1977 were erased. The 24-year downtrend from the 1977 high progressed in an orderly fashion. Each support level provided resistance in later years, and they should be expected to play an important role in the future. I thought cocoa had bottomed in 1992. Here, the downward thrust shortened, prices had returned to the top of the 1947 resistance line, and they were testing the vertical, liftoff area of 1973. Although prices had almost doubled by 1998, the up-move was too laborious. Notice the lack of upward follow-through after the minor breakout in 1997. In 1999, cocoa experienced an unrelenting down-move that ended with a close near the 1992 low.

A distinct change in behavior occurred in 2000. Here, we see little downward progress but no willingness to rally. Prices narrowed into the tightest yearly range since 1971. (Remember, the semilog scale draws larger price bars whenever prices decline. Thus, a cursory examination of the chart might lead one to believe the ranges in 1987 and 1996 were smaller than in 2000; however, this is not true.) In light of our discussion of narrow ranges, the behavior in 2000 deserves special attention. The market simply treaded water just below the 1992 low and the long-term uptrend line. The breaking of a trend line is not of major consequence by itself. What matters is how the trend line is broken and the amount of follow-through. As you see, there is no ease of downward movement. If the sellers still had the upper hand, prices should have continued lower. In the following year, when prices reversed above the 2000 high, the change of trend became obvious. After the rise above the 2000 high, one could have purchased cocoa with impunity. Over the next two years, cocoa prices rose over 200 percent. The behavior during 1992–2001 is typical of bottoms on charts constructed from any time period.

On the yearly cocoa and soybean oil charts, the price action around the major support/resistance lines told the main story. On the monthly bond chart (Figure 3.8), the story is different. Here, we see a reverse trend channel (dashed lines) that most aptly depicted the angle of advance in bond futures. It was drawn across the 1986–1993 highs with a parallel line across the 1987 low. A second parallel line was drawn across the 1990 low, and it provided support in 1994 and January 2000. Since it was first drawn, the lower parallel line has never interacted with price. The rallies in 1998 and 2003 penetrated the upper line of the reverse trend channel, creating a temporarily overbought condition. A reverse trend line and/or trend channel often fits best on those trends with the steepest angle of advance/decline. A normal trend channel drawn from the 1981 or 1984 lows would never have contained the subsequent price work. After prices rallied from the 1994 low, however, a normal trend channel could have been drawn across the 1987–1994 lows with a parallel line across the 1993 high. It fits nicely with the reverse trend channel. I prefer the reverse trend channel because it depicts the original angle of advance; its message was reinforced by the normal channel. The confluence of three upper-channel lines at the 2003 top warned that the bond market was grossly overbought. These three lines played an important role throughout the course of the uptrend.

The dramatic sell-off in 1987, coinciding with the stock market crash, found support on top of the 1982–1983 highs. Prices later consolidated on top of the resistance line drawn across the 1986 high. One can easily visualize the three-year apex that came to a conclusion in 1997. The uppermost resistance line drawn across the 1998 high (caused by the debacle in Long Term Capital Management) halted the rally in 2001. The nine months of pumping action between August 2002 and April 2003 marked the beginning of a five-year trading range. In December 2008, as the stock market went into a tailspin, bonds soared to 143, an unheard-of price until 2012. Bonds then traded in a volatile, 26-point range until the breakout in September 2011 reached 147. This high touched the same reverse trend lines as at the 2003 top.

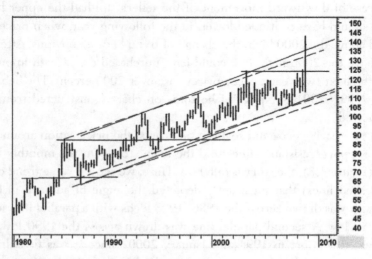

FIGURE 3.8 Bond Continuation Monthly Chart
Source: MetaStock.

In the modern-day Wyckoff course, the line of support across the bottom of a trading range is compared to the ice covering a frozen pond. It is called the *ice line*. Wyckoff never used this term, but it provides a memorable metaphor. The 1977–2000 downtrend on the cocoa yearly chart (Figure 3.7) demonstrates price repeatedly interacting with previous support or ice lines. A much smaller example appears in Figure 3.4 of soybean oil. Support line G drawn between the two highs served as a minor ice line. There were numerous attempts to rally upward from below line G, but no sustained advance developed.

One of the best examples of price interacting with an ice line occurred after the QQQ (Figure 3.9) made its all-time high. The QQQ experienced a sharp, high-volume break in January 2000 but then managed to make a series of new highs. After the February liftoff, the QQQ spent 10 days consolidating on top of the January trading range. It pushed off this former resistance level and climbed to the top of the up-channel on March 10 (point 1) where the daily range narrowed and the stock closed near the day's low. It looked tired and fell back to the March 16 low. Previously, on the 15th (point 2), the stock broke on the heaviest down-volume in its history. Volume failed to expand on the subsequent rally to the March 24 (point 3) top where we see the overbought position within the up-channel, the midrange close and the diminished upward progress (beyond the March 10 high). The buyers make a feeble attempt to lift prices on the following day (narrow range, low volume, and weak close) and the stock falls for three consecutive sessions toward the bottom of the current trading range. On April 3 (point 4), the QQQ falls with widening price spread and increased volume through the ice line drawn across the March 16 low and below the January high. The size of the daily range and volume set new records yet the buyers, who had become conditioned to take advantage of weakness, rushed in to drive prices toward the day's high and above the ice line. Despite the intraday recovery, the 32-point break from the March 24 high marked an overtly bearish change in behavior. It was followed by a low-volume rally that retraced less than 50 percent of the previous decline. The downward reversal on April 10 (point 5) ended the rally above the ice line, and prices dropped 29 points in five days. Notice how prices stabilized in April around the support line drawn across the January low. By then, however, 35 percent of the stock's value had been lost in 16 days. The speed and magnitude of its fall heralded the beginning of a major trend change. Although the peak was complete, the interaction with the ice line continued for six more months.

The lines shown in Figure 3.9 tell a larger story when extended across the weekly QQQ chart (Figure 3.10). Here, we see the stock struggle for

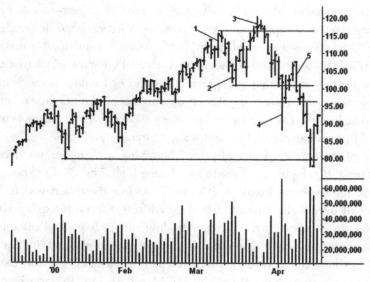

FIGURE 3.9 QQQ Daily Chart
Source: TradeStation.

six weeks during April and May to rally off the January support line. The sellers temporarily overcome the buyers and drive the stock below this support, but the lack of follow-through produces a big reversal. It leads to a test of the original ice line. After a second pullback, in late July, the stock makes another run at the ice line. The close for the week ending September 1, 2000,

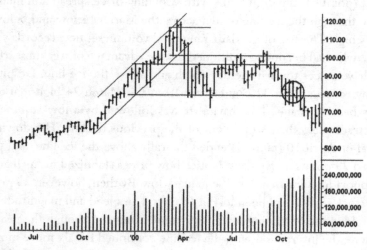

FIGURE 3.10 QQQ Weekly Chart
Source: TradeStation.

holds above the ice; however, the lack of follow-through plus the downward reversal in the following week underscore the sellers' dominance. Prices return to the bottom of the trading range (circled area) where the buyers and sellers lock into a five-week slugfest. It marked the buyers' last hope. The buying came from shorts liquidating positions established around the April–May lows, profit taking by traders who sold short in early September, and bottom picking by new longs. The sellers absorbed the buying, the topping process ended, and the downtrend began in earnest. While the March low has been labeled an ice line, the same metaphor can be applied to the line drawn across the January low. In fact, support lines drawn across the bottom of any trading range—on a yearly or an hourly chart—can be viewed in this light. Over the long-term, we should expect the January 2000 ice line to play a significant role in all of the Nasdaq indices. In fact, the rise from the 2009 low stopped against this line in 2012.

Throughout this book, we will see many more examples of price interacting with various types of lines and channels. But one more interaction needs to be described. The man who introduced the Wyckoff course to me always stressed the importance of apexes. He did not view apexes as so-called "continuation patterns." In fact, he did not concern himself with pattern recognition at all. Instead, he looked for price tightening and especially at or near the point of two converging trend lines. By itself, an apex has little or no predictive value. It simply indicates the amplitude of price swings has narrowed to a point of equilibrium between the forces of supply and demand. This equilibrium cannot continue indefinitely; it will be shattered. One looks for price/volume clues that indicate the future direction. Often, the evidence conflicts until some unusual volume surge or reversal action tips the scale in favor of one side. Wyckoff described behavior that foretells market direction out of dullness. He wrote:

> When a dull market shows its inability to hold rallies, or when it does not respond to bullish news, it is technically weak. . . . On the other hand, when there is a gradual hardening in prices; when bear raids fail to dislodge considerable quantities of stock; when stocks do not decline upon unfavorable news, we may look for an advancing market in the near future.[2]

Apexes on long-term charts (monthly, yearly) can be especially frustrating, but they offer the greatest reward. Between the late 1960s and 1980, my friend/mentor sought out these kinds of situations. Prior to changes in

[2] Rollo Tape [pseud.], *Studies in Tape Reading* (Burlington, VT: Fraser, 1910), 104.

the tax code regarding futures trading, he earned long-term capital gains by holding contracts for six months or more. This required purchasing deferred contracts and holding on with great tenacity. Often, the positions had to be rolled several times before the expected price move occurred. Like Wyckoff, he based much of his long-term forecasts on a battery of point–figure charts.

One of the most memorable and drawn-out apexes occurred in silver futures (Figure 3.11) between 1974 and 1977. Because of the bullish trend of commodities, few traders doubted that silver would ultimately move upward out of its trading range, but no one knew which up-move was the "real" one. With such a consensus of bullish expectations, it was the market's job to wear out as many longs as possible. Each upswing attracted a new herd of speculators who were promptly run out on the subsequent downswing. Yet clues emerged—mostly on the daily bar chart—that the buyers were steadily overcoming the sellers. On the monthly chart, unusual volume appeared in November–December 1976. Prices did not fall below the lows of this period until many years later. In 1977, silver found support in June. Although this low was washed out in August, prices ended the month in midrange. Volume in August 1977 was the lowest in over a year; it said the selling pressure was exhausted. Prices rose gently for two months and narrowed during November–December into the point of the apex.

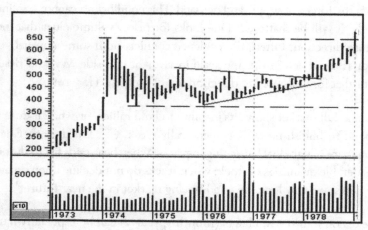

FIGURE 3.11 Silver Continuation Monthly Chart

The "breakout" from this apex occurred in the most lackluster manner possible: a narrow-range month followed by another month of lateral movement. Like a heavily laden truck, it lumbered out of the garage. The up-move in March 1978 saw widening price spread as prices exceeded the 1975 high, but there was no vertical liftoff. Compare the price action in January–February 1974 with the price rise during 1978. The vertical price rise in the first two months of 1974 reflects panic buying, a speculative blow-off—what Wyckoff referred to as *hypodermics*. No fanfare, no excitement accompanied the price rise in 1978. It produced doubt rather than eagerness to buy. Prices inched higher, testing and retesting every support/resistance level as the buyers gradually overcame the persistent selling. The quantities of silver offered at each resistance level were steadily absorbed as the ownership of the metal moved from weak hands to strong hands. The slow price movement in silver resembled, in many ways, the action one sees on a one-minute or five-minute bar chart. Tape readers have long recognized the significance of slow rallies as opposed to effervescent bubbles where prices levitate upward. Think of Wyckoff's "gradual hardening of price." Addressing this behavior, Humphrey Neill wrote, "A more gradual advance with constant volume of transactions, as opposed to spurts and wide price-changes, indicates a better quality of buying."[3] I should add that gradual advances attract short sellers, who perceive the slow pace to be a sign of weak demand, and who, when forced to cover, provide the fodder for additional price gains. In summation, the breakout from the four-year apex on the monthly silver chart did not begin with a loud thunderclap announcing the start of a new uptrend. Instead, it began as a crawl and eventually steamrolled into one of the biggest bull markets in the history of the futures markets.

We have just examined the classic apex unfolding over several years. Smaller apexes abound. They are drawn with a simple triangulation of trend lines to show prices at a nexus. Sometimes the triangulation is meaningful, other times not. But it helps to highlight a point of contraction such as the two on Figure 3.12 of Schlumberger (SLB).

The first apex (point 1) formed over a few days during September 1998 and requires no larger context; it stands alone. The larger apex (point 2) spanned four months, and we better understand its significance when we see its position on the weekly chart (Figure 3.13). Does the price/volume behavior within this apex portend further weakness or the beginning of a new uptrend? The total volume for the week ending December 4, 1998, is the largest on the chart; it is climactic. On the daily chart, we see the huge effort

---

[3] Humphrey B. Neill, *Tape Reading and Market Tactics* (Burlington, VT: Fraser Publishing, 1970), 118.

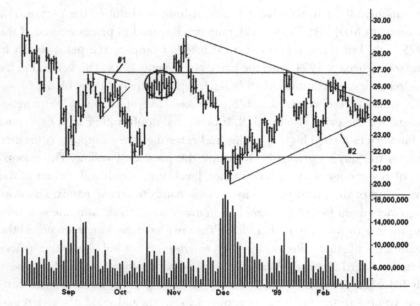

FIGURE 3.12 Schlumberger Daily Chart
Source: TradeStation.

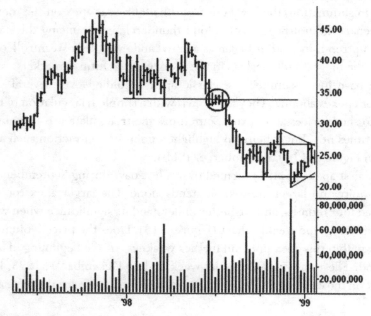

FIGURE 3.13 Schlumberger Weekly Bar Chart
Source: TradeStation.

to drive prices below the trading range. Yet there was little follow-through, and the stock quickly bobbed back into the trading range. All of the selling that emerged during the week of December 4 was erased on the ensuing rebound. On the weekly chart, a selling climax occurred in early December.

In the context of the daily chart, where we observe the details of the trading range from the September 1998 low, the high-volume plunge in December led to an upward reversal. It produced a rally to the top of the trading range. The lower volume on the pullback to the January low was a secondary test of the low. As prices lifted off the January low, one might have recognized that prices were narrowing into an apex. Lines would have been drawn across the November–January highs and the December–January lows to frame the price movement. The quick rise in early January and again in early February reflects the buyers' eagerness. Then the stock pulls back to the uptrend line and comes to rest above the January low.

In the last 8 weeks shown in Figure 3.14, prices tighten into a 2.25-point range. It says something is about to happen soon. The stock may start to lift out of the apex and reverse downward, or it may break downward and then reverse upward. If we buy the breakout or sell the breakdown, our risk increases and we make ourselves vulnerable to a whipsaw. The selling climax

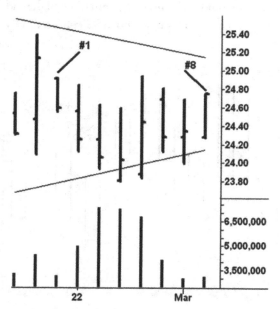

FIGURE 3.14 Schlumberger Daily Chart (Enlarged)
Source: TradeStation.

in early December, the reversal from the December low, and the stock's ability to make higher supports all paint a bullish story. Now let's read the message of the last eight price bars.

On days 1 through 4, prices close lower and near their lows. Volume increases on days 3 and 4. Note that the closes on days 3 through 5 are clustered within a 44-cent range, indicating little reward despite the large selling effort. The rally on day 5 erases most of the previous four days' losses, and the big increase in volume indicates the presence of demand. Over the next three days, prices narrow within the range of day 5, and volume dwindles. The closes on days 5 through 7 are bunched within a 31-cent range as the stock comes to dead center. The chart says go long on day 8 and protect below the low of day 4. SLB opens at 25 on March 3, kicking off a rally to 44. Price/volume behavior at the point of an apex is not always so perfect. Many times, one has to deal with a more ambiguous situation. In those instances, the behavior preceding the point of the apex usually determines the outcome.

As already mentioned, price tightness is the hallmark of an apex. When it occurs on yearly charts, the effect can be most dramatic. One of the greatest examples of this occurred on the yearly sugar chart (Figure 3.15), where cash prices coiled for four years within the year 2000 range. At the time, I thought nearby futures prices would rebound to 16 cents, the high made in the 1990s. As it turned out, cash and futures rose above 35 cents a few years later.

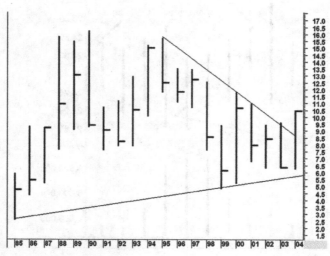

FIGURE 3.15 Cash Sugar Yearly Chart
Source: MetaStock.

Now we turn to an incomplete apex on Figure 3.16, the weekly chart of Home Depot. As shown, when I approach a chart for the first time, I dissect it by drawing the appropriate lines and highlighting those features that stand out the most. Here, we see prices rallied in late 1999 above an up-channel drawn from the 1998 low, and we make the following observations:

1. The vertical price rise during the first two weeks of December 1999 where the volume in the second week is the heaviest since the 1998 low.
2. The sell-off in the first week of January 2000 is the largest down week in years and is accompanied by the heaviest down-volume since the 1998 low.
3. The great ease of upward movement on the mid-March rally where the position of the closes in the circled area warn of impending trouble.
4. The tiny upthrust and huge downward reversal during the second week of April.
5. Support forms in May on top of the April–July 1999 resistance line.
6. The small upthrust of the July 2000 high is followed by a downward reversal on the largest daily volume during the second week of August.

Together, these elements tell a bearish story. Over the next few weeks, prices tighten into an apex between the downtrend line from the high and the uptrend line from the May 2000 low.

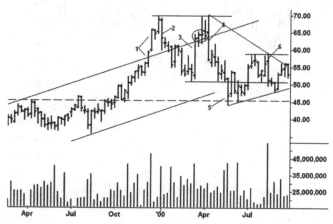

FIGURE 3.16 Home Depot Weekly Chart
Source: TradeStation.

The details of the apex are on the Home Depot daily chart (Figure 3.17). Here, we see a narrow trading range spanning 16 days. It has formed within the wide range (point 6) on the weekly chart. On day 9, prices break below the bottom of the range, but no follow-through selling emerges. This low is tested on day 13, where the stock closes on the low. Once again, the sellers fail to take advantage of bearish price action. The stock rallies on day 15 above the trading range but slips a bit on the close. No more buying power exists as the stock breaks on the last day and closes below the bar 15 low. The down-volume on the last day is the largest since the August low. Now we have a sequence of behavior to act upon. No one knows for certain if the trading range will continue and prices coil further into the apex. But the minor upthrust in the context of an oppressively bearish weekly chart increases the likelihood of a breakdown. Shorts are established on the close or the opening of the following day and stops placed above the high of day 15. On the next day, the stock fell to 51.12. Four days later it hit 35, where the enormous volume signaled climactic action. I realize that some of the twists and turns within the small trading range appeared bullish at times. But the stalling of the market in the area where supply last overcame demand (point 6) was the overriding consideration. It should have kept one fixed on the idea of looking for a shorting opportunity rather than making a quick long trade.

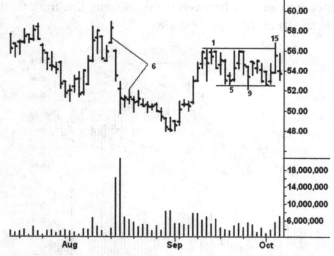

FIGURE 3.17   Home Depot Daily Chart
Source: TradeStation.

In the study of Schlumberger and Home Depot, I am leading the reader beyond the mere story of the lines. I have integrated the story of the lines with the bar-by-bar chart reading that incorporates a comparison of price range, position of the close, and volume. There's much more ahead.

CHAPTER 4

The Logic of Reading Bar Charts

Wflhen studying a bar chart, we go through a process of sequential
evaluation. This normally consists of comparing the immediate price
movement with the most recent price bars. From this comparison, we make
deductions or inferences about what to expect in the next time period. Of
course, we are always faced with the realization that anything can happen.
The market we are watching can gap sharply higher or lower because of
unexpected news events. These are the extremes of the probability curve,
but they must be accepted as part of the territory by anyone who ventures
into speculation.. The exercise below is purely abstract. No contextual
clues such as trend lines, channels, support/resistance levels, and volume
are provided. Let's assume two things: each vertical bar represents one day
and prices are in a downtrend. The first bar is day "a" and the second is "b."
From this minimal information, what do you expect to happen on day "c"?
I realize there are always two interpretations (the glass is either half full or
half empty), but what is your best deduction? There may be some instances
where the situation is too ambiguous. Consider the price range and the position of the close. Do not consider these two-bar sequences as "cookie prints"
for studying future price movement. We are examining the price behavior of
two days in order to construct a logical set of expectations for the following
day. My observations and deductions are included.

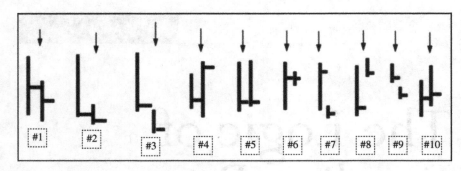

FIGURE 4.1 Sequential Chart Reading

Figure 4.1, #1: The size of bar "a" reflects ease of downward movement and it describes what is meant by a large bar Since the close is in the middle of the range, we assume buying emerged at the lower levels of the day. On day "b," the range narrows, thus reflecting no ease of downward movement. The low of the day is only slightly below the low of day "a" as the thrust shortens. Finally, the close is again midrange, indicating that buyers were present at lower levels.

For two consecutive days, prices closed in midrange and the downward thrust shortened. The market is displaying an unwillingness to move lower. Therefore, expect an attempt to rally on day "c." If the rally exceeds the top of day "b," and prices then reverse below the low of day "b," expect further weakness.

Figure 4.1, #2: There is ease of downward movement on day "a," and the close at the low of the range reflects a total victory by the sellers. The narrow range on day "b" is more difficult to interpret. Does it mean the sellers were unable to make much headway? Does it mean the buyers made a stand and took all of the sellers' offers? The position of the close gives us a better clue. Since the close is on the low of day "b" and below the low of day "a," we infer the sellers are still in control. If the close had been at the high of the range, the outcome would have tilted more in favor of the bulls.

Given the position of the close on day "b" we tentatively expect further weakness on day "c." If there is little or no downward follow-through on day "c" and prices rally above the high of day "b," larger gains are likely.

Figure 4.1, #3: Day "a" personifies weakness: ease of downward movement and a close near the low of the range. A small gap lower occurs on day "b," but the range narrows. The close on day "b" is near the low and below the previous day's close and low.

Although there was no ease of downward movement on day "b," all of the trading took place below the previous day's low. There was no ability to rally. In addition, the day ended with a close on the low. The sellers remain in control so expect lower prices. Should price reverse above the close of day "a"—especially after falling below the low of day "b"—a turnaround of some unknown degree would occur. This two-day configuration is more bearish than #1 or #2.

Figure 4.1, #4: The price range is narrower on day "a," and the close is near the low of the range. Thus, the sellers were seemingly in control at the end of day "a." On day "b," price falls below the previous day's low and reverses to close above the previous day's high.

The reversal action on day "b" is the classic *key reversal.* It tells us there was no further selling interest below the previous low. The lack of selling pressure created a vacuum and the buyers stepped in. Much of this buying may have been short covering. But the strong close above the previous day's high suggests support has at least temporarily formed. One would expect upward follow-through on day "c." A reversal and close below the low of day "b" would be very bearish. The low of day "b" can be used as a stop point on any new long.

Figure 4.1, #5: There is ease of downward movement on day "a" and the close is near the low of the range. On day "b," a rally above the previous day's high fails to hold and prices fall back to close near the low. The closes on the two days are just about equal. Would you think the clustering of these two closes reflects strong support?

Because the rally on day "b" failed to hold and 99 percent of the gains were erased on the close, we would expect further weakness on day "c." Here, we have two consecutive days of holding action, but the position of the closes reflects weakness and an inability to sustain a rally. No, the clustering of these two closes would not normally be viewed as strong support. It looks more like temporary support in a downtrend.

Figure 4.1, #6: Although there is ease of downward movement on day "a," the position of the close is well off the low and much nearer the high. Day "b" is one of those inscrutable, narrow-range bars where prices barely budge from the previous day's close.

The position of the close on day "a" indicates buying appeared at the lower level of the range. It has a bullish connotation. Day "b" shows a total lack of movement. In the Wyckoff lexicon, this kind of day is referred to as a "hinge" from which a larger swing may occur. In the context of these two days, the hinge says prices have come to dead center. It alone does not reveal direction, but it tells us to be very alert on day "c" for something decisive.

Figure 4.1, #7: As in the preceding example, there is ease of downward movement on day "a," and the close is near the high of the range. Day "b," however, contains a large gap between its high and the close of the previous day. The actual range is narrow, and price closes near the low and below the previous day's low.

Although the actual range on day "b" is narrow, the true range—encompassing the gap—is quite large. Here, we see all of the gains made on day "a" completely erased. The gap probably stems from bearish overnight events or a preopening report. Notice how little movement occurred after the gap opening. This reflects a bearish condition as the buyers were unwilling to make any attempt to start a move on the upside. Nor were the sellers eager to take profits. The selling pressure and lack of buying kept prices depressed throughout the session. Expect further weakness on day "c."

Figure 4.1, #8: Here we have the reverse of #7. We see ease of downward movement on day "a," with a weak close near the low of the range. On day "b," price gaps higher and rallies above the high of the previous day; however, the close is on the low of the actual range and slightly below the high of day "a."

The true range of day "b" begins from the close of day "a." Some unexpectedly bullish news caused such a gap higher. The action on day "b" is decidedly bullish as it erases all of the previous day's weakness. Except for the position of the close, it rates in bullishness next to the key reversal in #4. One might be concerned about the "weak" close on day "b." But it is not weak when we consider the true range.

Figure 4.1, #9: Both days "a" and "b" have narrow ranges and close near their lows. On day "b," price opens below the low of the previous day and stays below its low throughout the entire session.

We see no ease of downward movement on either day. These two price bars reflect a steadily eroding market in which the buyers are backing away. The volume is probably low to moderate. No wild, flailing, climactic action here. Instead, we have two slow, steady, unobtrusive down days (slip-sliding away) with the few upticks most likely caused by light short covering or a few foolhardy bottom pickers. Expect further weakness on day "c."

Figure 4.1, #10: The range of day "a" does not reflect great ease of downward movement and price closes in the middle. On day "b," price rallies with somewhat greater ease but closes well off the high of the day, below the high of day "a" and only a fraction higher.

The midrange close on day "a" and the lack of a wide price spread suggest buying is present. At the end of day "a," a rally would have seemed likely.

A robust rally occurs on day "b," but the position of the close indicates selling was encountered. The close of day "b" marks the midpoint of the two days' trading. We can assume trading has been brisk, possibly volatile; however, little upward progress is achieved. The sellers still appear in control; therefore, expect weakness on day "c." Depending on where day "c" opens, the information here could quickly fit into an equally bullish or bearish story. In many ways, #10 represents the most ambiguous situation.

In Figure 4.2, I have arranged the 10, 2-day sequences discussed above into a 20-day decline. The order remains exactly the same. While this is a purely hypothetical situation, created randomly, it has a realistic look with a typical mixture of clarity and ambiguity. I have drawn support/resistance lines and a normal downtrend channel connecting two highs and an intervening low. Together these lines frame the price movement. They help tell the story about where minor trading ranges formed and where the breakdowns occurred; they highlight the false breakouts/breakdowns and the angle of decline.

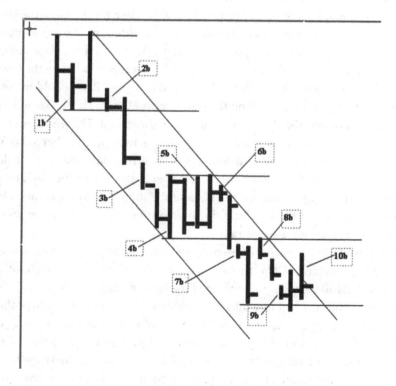

FIGURE 4.2 Hypothetical Price Movement

When viewed in a larger context, some of the price bars take on a new meaning. The price action at the close of bar 1b pointed to a rally. As we see, the resulting rally upthrusted the top of 1a. and price reversed downward in a bearish manner. We recognized the bearish connotations for bar 2b and here it becomes more apparent as the market hugs its low with no ability to rally. The ease of downward movement in 3a shows the sellers have gained the upper hand and they remain dominant in 3b and 4a. The key reversal in 4b temporarily stops the sell-off. The price action in 5a and 5b paints a bearish picture. In 6a, however, the firm close says the buyers are trying to absorb the overhead selling. Price comes to dead center in 6b and we wait for the market to show its hand. As usual, it is tricky and volatile. In 7a, the bottom of the immediate trading range is penetrated yet price reverses upward. This spring-like action had bullish potential as long as the low of 7a held. As it turned out, some bearish overnight development caused a sharply lower gap opening on 7b. Once again the implication was very bearish and prices accelerated lower on 8a. When we looked at day 8b as part of a two-day exercise, the recovery appeared bullish. On this chart, however, we see 8b as an attempt to move above the former support line. The position of the close on 8b warns the effort has failed. The narrow ranges in 9a and 9b reflect little ease of movement and suggest a secondary test of the recent low. Day 10a, which seemed so ambiguous in abstract form, looks more meaningful here. Price falls below the low of the trading range and there is little downward progress. If we could measure the amount of ground covered on the down-moves below 1b, 4b, 8a, and 10a, it would be obvious the downward thrust has shortened. The position of the close is midrange and above the close of 9b. It says to expect further gains. On the final day, 10b, price rallies through the downtrend line; however, it does not resolve the situation because the close is near the low of the day's range. But price did manage to exceed the highs of the three previous bars and close fractionally higher. If there is little downward pressure on 11a, price will be on the springboard for a larger rally.

So far, we have referred to ease of movement, springs, upthrusts, absorption, and shortening of the thrust. They will be discussed throughout the chapters that follow. Volume is the one missing ingredient. In order to incorporate the subject of volume into this discussion, I have plotted a hypothetical volume histogram below the price bars. Because these charts are drawn manually, the spacing between each day is not perfectly equidistant. While the chart may not have a great deal of graphic precision, the behavior herein complements the other elements we have discussed. But first a few words about volume, which measures force. We compare the force (or effort) of the buying and selling against the reward (price gain or loss) to determine which side is dominant and to identify signs of an imminent change in trend. Volume interpretation is routinely reduced to a set of general formulas: price and volume rising = bullish; price rising and volume falling = bearish; price falling and volume rising = bearish, price falling and volume falling = bullish. These formulas are too simplistic. They do not capture the nuance of price/volume behavior. They only serve as rough guidelines. For example, there are occasions when price rises on decreasing volume because fewer traders want to bet against a strong uptrend. Conversely, many times prices fall on diminished volume because the buyers have backed away or given up. Rallies and sell-offs on very heavy volume can indicate climactic or stopping action. Rallies and sell-offs on very low volume often signify exhaustion. Many trends begin with a burst of volume, which serves as the prime mover, the impetus for a larger swing. After this initial burst of energy, volume often dwindles. Wyckoff's eloquent description of market forces is instructive:

> The market is like a slowly revolving wheel: Whether the wheel will continue to revolve in the same direction, stand still or reverse depends entirely upon the forces which come in contact with it hub and tread. Even when the contact is broken, and nothing remains to affect its course, the wheel retains a certain impulse from the most recent dominating force, and revolves until it comes to a standstill or is subjected to other influences.[1]

Volume is best interpreted in conjunction with the price range and the position of the close. In Figure 4.3, the bearishness of the upthrust and downward reversal on 2a is underscored by the heavy selling pressure reflected in the large volume. The breakdown on 3a, where we see ease of downward movement and a weak close, tells a bearish story by itself. The large volume as prices fall below support indicates that the force of the selling has overcome the force of the buying. On 3b and 4a, prices glide lower on modest volume. Here, the low volume—like the weak closes—indicates a lack of demand. The heavy volume on 4b reinforces the key reversal. Yet volume fails to show aggressive demand on 5a, 5b, and 6a as prices pump up and down in a small range. A large selling effort on 7a is overcome by buying as price recovers. The lack of reward for the effort would suggest that the buyers are gaining the upper hand. Then the bearish news hits the market on 7b, and price gaps below the previous low. The selling reaches a crescendo on 8a, but the weak close

---

[1] Rollo Tape [pseud.], *Studies in Tape Reading* (Burlington, VT: Fraser, 1910), 13.

still warns of lower prices. There is no downward progress on 8b as price gaps higher; however, it fails to clear the previous support line drawn across the low of 4b. The previous support line serves as resistance. But we cannot ignore the fact the volume on this up day is the second heaviest of any up day on the chart.

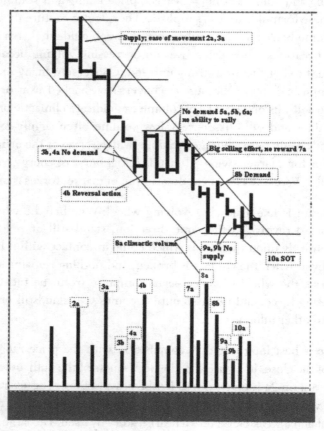

FIGURE 4.3 Hypothetical Behavior

One can construct a story that buyers may have begun to emerge under cover of climactic volume on 8a. When a market is full of selling, buying often goes undetected. Demand appeared on 8b but it was not sufficient to break through the overhead resistance. It is the price/volume behavior on 9a and 9b—narrow ranges and low volume—that suggests the selling pressure is tiring. (One might question why 9a and 9b are not interpreted bearishly like 3b and 4a. The latter two days are in the midst of a decline. The former two days were on a retest of a high-volume low.) But because the closes on 9a and 9b remain close to their lows, a washout of 8a is still possible. This occurs on 10a. The diminished volume on 10a is noteworthy. Since the entire down-move began, this marks the lowest volume on a penetration of support. (Compare it with 3a and 8a.) The position of the close on 10a is near midrange, and, more important, above the low of 8a. It says the selling pressure is spent. On one level, the action on 10a represents a minor spring of 8a. In the context of the entire down-move, we see shortening of the thrust (SOT) on 10a. Much of the gain on 10b is erased on the close. If this were a real trading situation, one would watch the character of the pullback from the high of 10b to see if the selling pressure is spent. If the volume contracts, a low-risk buying opportunity exists. Another buying strategy would be to go long on a stop above the high of 10b.

Now let's look at the Standard & Poor's (S&P) continuation chart in 2003. Figure 4.4 shows 17 days of price work beginning in the midst of an uptrend. What behavior most dominated the price movement? I am not referring to one particular day. I am not referring to trend lines or the volume. I am not referring to the market's ability to make higher highs and lows. What behavior has repeatedly occurred to allow the uptrend to continue? Subliminally, you know the answer. You only need to know the concept.

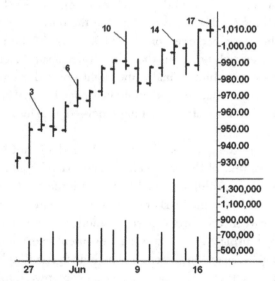

FIGURE 4.4 S&P Daily Continuation Chart
Source: TradeStation.

What is the most bearish behavior on the S&P chart (Figure 4.4)? How do you interpret the meaning of days 16 and 17 in the context of the overall chart? What do you expect to occur on day 18? What nearby price level would have to be penetrated to indicate that the sellers are gaining the upper hand? If you were long, where would you place a protective stop? Assume you went long on day 12. These are the kinds of questions we ask ourselves as we look over a chart.

From my perspective, the uptrend in Figure 4.4 is sustained by the buyers' repeated ability to overcome all selling efforts. Expressed another way, whenever the sellers had an opportunity to drive prices lower, they lost it. There was little or no downward follow-through. Days 3 and 4 illustrate the point. The narrowing of the price range and the position of the close suggested that demand was tired after the big up-move on day 2. The market probably encountered profit taking by longs. Thus, day 3 warned of a correction. Day 4 increased the likelihood of a deeper pullback. Here, the market rallied above the previous day's high, reversed below the previous day's low, and closed on a weak note. The advantage had seemingly shifted to the sellers. Yet the lack of follow-through on day 5 prompted new buying and the uptrend resumed. After racing upward on days 5 and 6, traders again took profits. Note the position of the close on day 6, which says the market encountered selling. The lack of follow-through selling on day 7 set the stage for an additional round of buying. Again, we see that the market encountered selling on day 10, as reflected in the position of the close. The most bearish behavior occurred on day 11 as most of the previous three days' gains were erased; however, the sellers once again failed to capitalize on the market's vulnerability. Finally, the slight upward progress and small gain on day 14 warned that demand might be tiring. The market gave ground easily on day 15, but no sustained selling emerged as price surged to a new high on day 16.

This brings us to the question about days 16 and 17, not in the abstract, but within the context of the entire chart. The sharp break on days 10 and 11 can be likened to a soldier's wound. It's not a mortal wound, but it requires time to heal. Thus, the market rests or consolidates in a trading range. The balance between the forces of supply and demand shifts on day 16. Here, the market displays ease of upward movement, closes on the high, and closes at the highest price on the chart. The bullish flag flies high again; the bulls reign. Day 17, however, raises concerns: little upward follow-through, narrow price range, and a midrange close. This warns that demand may be spent. A narrow price range on a move to new highs should not be disregarded, as it often leads to weakness.

On day 18 (Figure 4.5), the S&P failed to exceed the previous day's high and fell below its low. The close softened the bearish message by ending in midrange and slightly lower. Still, we have to be concerned with the narrow ranges that suggest an upthrust has occurred. The flip side of the argument says the market is undergoing absorption. On a retest of a previous resistance level, the buyers must absorb the liquidation by longs who bought on day 10, the profit taking by longs who bought at lower levels, and the new short selling attracted to the high price. Therefore, we have to weigh the potential upthrust against the possibility that absorption may be taking place. Anyone long should raise stops to below the low of day 18.

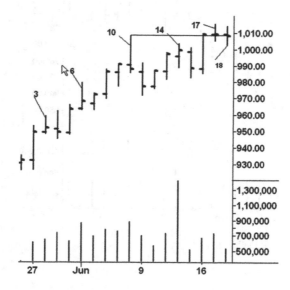

FIGURE 4.5   S&P Daily Chart 2
Source: TradeStation.

The answer becomes apparent on day 19 (Figure 4.6). After a brief attempt to rally on the opening, the S&P plunged below the lows of the past two days. Much of the gains made on day 16 are erased. Notice how the daily volumes all look the same and tell us little about the force of the buying and selling. We mostly have to rely on the size of the range and the position of the close to read the chart. The sellers have now gained the upper hand, and the breakout above the trading range was indeed an upthrust. The lesson here is simple: always be on guard when a market moves above previous highs and the range narrows. Determining the resolution of a trading range is made easier by more price history. For example, the break from the high of day 10 to the low of day 11 marked the largest two-day decline in over three months. This bearish change in behavior glared forth on the daily chart. Shorts established on a stop below day 18 would have been protected with a stop above the day 17 high. The stop should then be lowered to the high of day 19.

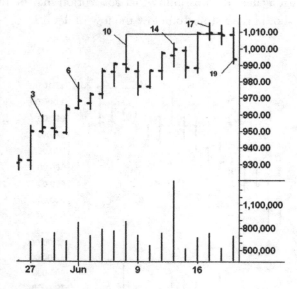

FIGURE 4.6 S&P Daily Chart 3
Source: TradeStation.

Figure 4.7 shows the next eight trading sessions. After day 21, the market makes little downward progress. The reversal action on day 23 looks quite threatening as prices close below the lower boundary of the trading range. Although there was no immediate follow-through selling, the market was unable to rally away from the danger point. When prices persistently hug the low of a trading range, the odds favor at least a washout and many times a sharp down-move. (Notice how days 24 through 26 hold within the range of day 23.) On day 27, the market fell below the lows of the previous six days and reversed upward into the trading range. This created a potential spring of the trading range that began from the high of day 10. The low on day 27 is in the "crisscross area" between the high of day 4 and the low of day 7 around the 962 line. Demand appeared on the up-move from day 7 and it re-emerged on day 27. We are viewing the chart like a tape reader, with attention given to where earlier struggles took place that may offer support on reactions.

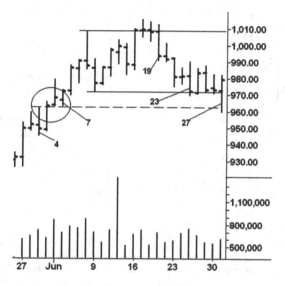

FIGURE 4.7 S&P Daily Chart 4
Source: TradeStation.

As shown in Figure 4.8, the spring on day 27 was tested two days later where the volume diminished and price closed well off the low. Demand returned on day 30, as indicated by the ease of upward movement and the strong close. On day 31, however, the range narrowed as the market approached the top of the range. Because of the firm close, it seemed that the buyers could be absorbing the overhead supply. Then we have a fairly mild outside downward reversal on day 32. The market gave further ground on day 33, but there is no downward follow-through on day 34. This opens the door for another test of the overhead resistance. On day 35, prices rally above the day 32 high but give ground and close near the low of the session. Supply has been encountered, as indicated by the weak price action and the increased volume. Day 36 seals the market's fate. Here, another attempt to clear resistance fails and the market closes nearer the low of the day. The odds favor another downswing. It continues until August 5 and ends with a spring of the day 27 low. From there, prices rise for six months.

FIGURE 4.8 S&P Daily Chart 5
Source: TradeStation.

A portion of the six-month uptrend is shown on Figure 4.9 of the Dow Jones Industrial Average. It begins from the November 21, 2003, low, the steepest phase of the uptrend. For this study, I have included a true range histogram below the price work. Its setting is one rather than a comparison with other days' readings. As you will see, daily ranges can be interpreted like volume; they serve as an excellent proxy for volume. The actual volume did not provide as much differentiation between high and low readings. I remember the day, January 2, 2004, when I noticed a change in behavior. On this day, the Dow had its first outside, downward reversal since the November low. Most notably, its range was the largest of any previous down-bar. I thought this was a bearish change in behavior; however, the following day erased all of this weakness. Five days later (1/9), the Dow sold off with another wide range. On January 13, we see another wide-range downward reversal. Notice how the declines on January 9 and 13 tested the January 2 range. Yet the position of the close on the 13th indicated the presence of buying. Over the next eight sessions, the Dow rallied 340 points. The pace of the move was more labored than the advance in December. But the big in-traday rally on January 21 spanned 153 points, the largest in several months. Another strong performance occurred on January 26. At first glance, the buyers seemed in total control. Yet there was no upward follow-through on the next day, and on January 28, the market suffered its largest intraday sell-off since April 2003, washing away all the gains made between January 21 and 26. This was a serious change in behavior. Bob Evans, the most well known of Wyckoff teachers, would say to put "a wad of peanut butter" on this bar so as to keep it foremost in mind. (A friend used to write the word *wad* in bold letters on his charts.) But the selling quickly abated, and prices held for six sessions in a narrow range.

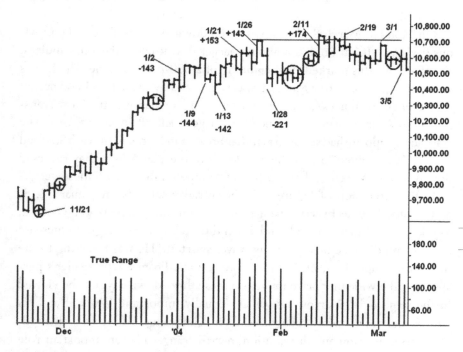

FIGURE 4.9 Dow Jones Industrial Average Daily Chart
Source: TradeStation.

The next upswing culminated with a strong performance on February 11, where the Dow gained 174 points from the low, closed on the high, and made a new high for the year. Although the buyers appeared in control, the rally stalled for five consecutive sessions. On the fifth day, February 19, the buyers pushed the market to a fractional new high before it reversed to close near the day's low. At this point, all of the behavior from January 2 came into focus and said to expect a larger sell-off. The buying effort on March 1 was totally erased the next day, where prices closed near the previous day's low. On March 3 and 4, the Dow held in narrow ranges. Their significance cannot be minimized. They mark the spot, dead center in the middle of the trading range, where, if the bulls were to regain control, the market must rally. On the surface, March 5 looks ambiguous: prices pumped up and down, settled in midrange and barely closed higher. Who won the struggle—the buyers or the sellers? We consider how the character of the up-move changed between January 13 and 26, the wide-open break on January 28, the buyers' lost opportunities after February 11 and March 1, and the upthrust on February 19. In this context, the indecisiveness on March 5 underscores the market's vulnerability.

On Monday, March 8, the Dow turned down and closed near the previous day's low. It left no doubt about a larger downturn in the stock indices. For the Dow, this marked the beginning of a 600-point decline. The Dow's vulnerable position after March 5 was reinforced by the action in several of the other stock indices/averages. For example, by March 5, the Dow Transportation Average had experienced its largest sell-off in over a year. The Nasdaq Composite had suffered a similar break. On March 5, the cash S&P and Russell 2000 rallied to their highest levels of the year. When they reversed downward on March 8, their upthrusts trumpeted the bearish message.

In the discussion of Figure 4.9, the intraday sell-offs on January 2, 9, and 28 stood out as bearish changes in behavior. In his tape reading course, Wyckoff stated that uptrends end when the "selling waves begin to increase in time and distance or the buying waves shorten." He was referring to the uptrend, or upswings, on intraday wave charts. From a tape reader's perspective, the widening price ranges on these three down days can be viewed in the same light. Narrow ranges are equally important. Wyckoff and his later associates certainly recognized their significance. Based on their models of accumulation and distribution, narrow ranges play an important role in defining the final turning point within a trading range prior to markup or markdown. Of course, as illustrated in the preceding discussion, narrow ranges tell us something about ease of movement—especially when we factor in the position of the close.

Narrow ranges play a major role in the analytical writings of Toby Crabel, the legendary trader/analyst who, after publishing a book dealing with his discoveries about the nature of markets, attempted to buy back each copy from the publisher. A few of these slipped through the cracks and quickly became rare books. In his book, *Day Trading with Short Term Price Patterns and Opening Range Breakout*, Toby Crabel cites the work of Arthur Merrill as a source of inspiration. But he also displays a thorough understanding of Wyckoff's concepts of the Last Point of Supply and Last Point of Support as the source for a particular narrow-range pattern. Crabel approaches Wyckoff from the perspective of a quantitative analyst. He tested day trading results based on buying or selling opening range breakouts from several combinations of narrow-range days. In a particularly salient passage, he wrote:

> It should be clarified that although these tests are presented in a rough system format, it is not advised that they be traded as such. The purpose of all my work is to determine the markets' nature. This market concept assists me with that. When applying the 2Bar NR [narrow range] (or any market concept), the full context of the market must be considered. I define market context as the integration of the trend, price action, price pattern studies, and support/resistance. The primary is the trend and [it] overrides all other particulars of market context.[2]

The 2Bar NR represents the narrowest two consecutive days range when compared to any two-day range during the last 20 market sessions. It represents what he calls the Principle of Contraction/Expansion, which explains how markets alternate between periods of activity and periods of rest. By prescribing a relative size rather than a specified size, the concept of 2Bar NR works in either volatile or dull market conditions. In Figure 4.9, a 2Bar NR occurred on March 3–4. Prior to the opening on March 5, we knew the market was in a position from which it had to rally. That the up-move on March 5 failed to hold adds to our understanding of the market's vulnerability. I have also circled two other instances of 2Bar NR. The action on February 9–10 did produce a one-day, bullish response. Crabel quantifies several other narrow price configurations. One notable pattern, the 3Bar NR, is defined as the narrowest three-day price range within the previous 20 market days. Regarding this pattern, he makes some insightful comments:

> The psychological implications of a pattern of this type [3Bar NR] are interesting. In general, as the pattern is forming, speculators are absent. In fact they tend to ignore a market that has contracted to such an extent. This is the point where the market is most ready to move and presents an explosive opportunity. It is ironic that so little initial interest is given to the move out of this pattern. It is well-trained traders that recognize these opportunities and provide for the force that takes the market into a trend. I suggest that the patterns be looked at

---

[2]Toby Crabel, *Day Trading with Short Term Price Patterns and Opening Range Breakout* Greenville, South Carolina, Traders Press, 1990), 164.

very carefully as they form in order to anticipate the upcoming action. Again the quantification of this pattern allows you to do just that. The tests show several things: 1) That there is a market tendency for the market to trend intraday the day after the pattern has formed; 2) That the overall trend of the market has an impact on the pattern's ability to continue the trend 2 to 5 days after the pattern has formed. This is different from the 2Bar NR which shows trending in the direction of the breakout regardless of the trend."[3]

On the Dow chart, a 3Bar NR formed during February 3–5. These three narrow days formed within the range of February 2. Since Crabel found Inside Days to be "precursors of trending action," this particular 3Bar NR had greater potential, as proven by the resulting 250-point rally. Wyckoff referred to such price tightness as a hinge. It can be likened to the hinge that allows a door to swing open. A hinge is the precursor to a price swing. A hinge on a weekly or monthly chart usually leads to many of the biggest swings. Crabel tested another narrow-range pattern called an NR4. It consists of a day with a daily range that is narrower than each of the previous three days ranges. Favorable test results were also observed when the NR4 occurred as an inside day (ID/NR4). This pattern appears less frequently than the NR4. An ID/NR4 occurred on December 24, but the holiday trading conditions diluted its impact. November 21 and 28 are typical of an NR4. The minor spring and position of the close on November 21 gave the NR4 a more compelling story. As we have seen, Wyckoff's method integrates price range, position of close, volume, and the interaction with support/resistance and trend lines to explain what is taking place on a chart. Crabel, however, focuses on a setup that will produce a trend day to allow a successful day trade or a 2- to 5-day swing. It often increases the immediacy of the more intuitive Wyckoff approach.

Crabel strives for specific day-trading rules. Wyckoff reads the struggle between buyers and sellers without hard-and-fast rules. For example, the four days between February 12 and 18 held within the range of the 11th. February 12 is the only ID/NR4. but it produced no trend day. Cumulatively, these four inside days put the burden of proof on the bears. This tightness said the market is not giving ground; the buyers are trying to absorb the overhead supply; watch the character of the next up-move. The poor performance on the following day shifted the story to

---

[3] Ibid., 177.

the bearish side. This is the way I prefer to combine Crabel's work with Wyckoff's methods.

With these thoughts in mind, we turn to U.S. Steel in the midst of an uptrend (Figure 4.10). In late October 2003, this stock jumped above the major resistance at 22. When demand overcame supply (D/S), the price ranges widened and volume increased. Upward progress slowed above 24. On November 5 (point 1), the reversal action warned of a correction. Two days later (point 2), the stock attempted to test the high; however, the range was narrower than any of the previous six days (NR7), and price closed unchanged in the middle. The breakdown on the next day called for further weakness. In the last four days of the decline, the price ranges narrow and volume contracts—ideal behavior on a test of a breakout. Long positions should be established on the next day's opening with a stop just below 20.95, the low of the bars where demand overcame supply. The last three days also meet the definition of a 3Bar NR. Here we have arrived at a point where both trading methods demand action. The price/volume behavior gives us the ideal pullback to test a breakout (cf. Figure 1.1, Where to Find Trades), and the 3Bar NR indicates to go long (short) on a specified number of points above (below) the opening range. Given the underlying bullish trend, a long position would be preferred.

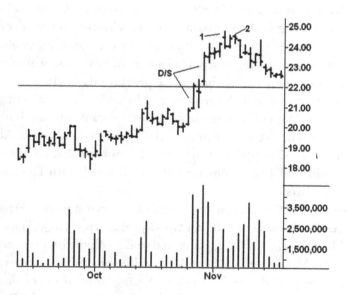

FIGURE 4.10 U.S. Steel Daily Chart
Source: TradeStation.

As you can see in Figure 4.11, U.S. Steel made higher highs, lows, and closes for six consecutive sessions. On the sixth day (12/1), the range expanded to 1.64 points, the largest since October 30 when the true range equaled 1.97 points. This ease of upward movement occurs on the breakout above the November high. The up-move stalled over the next three sessions as longs took profits. One would normally expect the stock to pull back and test the breakout. The shallow correction, however, gives no one an opportunity to buy more cheaply on weakness; it testifies to the underlying strength of the trend. As noted, Crabel considers inside days to be "precursors of trending action." These 3 days might be confused with a 3Bar NR, except 3 narrower days occurred within the last 20 days (at the November low). Again, given the shallowness of the ranges and the clustering of closes, the odds favor further upward progress. At first glance, day 3 looks disappointing. Here, the stock rallies above the highs of the previous four sessions and reverses to close unchanged and near the low of its range. In many ways, it looks like the behavior in the Dow on February 19 (Figure 4.9). But the cumulative behavior in that instance pointed to a downturn; not so in U.S. Steel. Within the bell-shaped curve of probabilities regarding the next day's performance, day 3 warns of a potential upthrust. Instead, the stock gaps higher on the next day (December 8)—almost above the high of point 3—and races upward with widening price spread (1.99-point true range) and a firm close. The strong gap opening is at the extreme of probabilities. Yet an alert trader must react immediately to the situation. As the stock races above the previous day's high, an aggressive trader should buy more shares and protect with a stop immediately below the previous day's close. There is no guarantee of success, but the sequence of behavior favors a continuation of the uptrend. While I have made no statistical study of such bullish lift-offs, my experience says the vast majority occur in an uptrend. Although the action on day 3 suggests an upthrust, it's not unusual for them to fail within an uptrend just as downtrends are littered with failed springs. More on this later.

The Principle of Contraction/Expansion can be seen at work in Figure 4.12. After December 8, the stock holds for two days in a narrow range. The second of these holds inside the first. Yet, compared to the volume on previous down-bars since the November low, here the down-volume is the heaviest. It indicates the presence of demand as the large selling effort makes no downward progress. Finally, notice how prices held both days on top of the December 8 high. Once again, we see shallow corrections that lock out would-be

FIGURE 4.11 U.S. Steel Daily Chart 2
Source: TradeStation.

buyers. The trend resumes (December 11) with a widening price range equaling 1.97 points. Here, the volume swells to the highest level since April. It may signal climactic action or the beginning of a steeper rise. We do know the stock has reached an overbought point within the up-channel. On December 12 (point 4), volume swells to an even higher level. The two days' combined volume could be indicative of a buying climax. A sell-off below the low of these two days (28.11) could threaten the uptrend, so stops on long positions are raised to 28.09.

U.S. Steel gaps higher on December 15 (Figure 4.13), with a true range equaling 1.26 points, the fourth largest since November 21. On the following day (point 5), the stock closes 55 cents lower, the largest loss since the up-move began. Incredibly, this also marks the first time the stock closed below a previous day's low. Yet, on December 17, the stock reverses upward to close above the highs of the past two days. After the strong performance on December 18, stops can be raised a few cents below 30.51, the low of the previous session. A steeper up-channel is drawn off the lows of December 11 (28.11) and December 17. As the uptrend progresses, we notice two inside days on December 23 and 24 (point 6). The latter is an NR7 and the stock holds on top of the December 18 high. Holiday trading conditions explain the low volume on the next day. On

FIGURE 4.12 U.S. Steel Daily Chart 3
Source: TradeStation.

December 29, the stock has another 1.97-point range and reaches the top of the up-channel. It then moves laterally for five sessions while holding on top of the previous high. Two of the five days warn of a larger correction. First and foremost is the price action on December 30. This stands out as the most bearish change in behavior since November 21. Here the stock had its largest intraday break and its largest loss—all on an inside day. Compare the price action on this day to the Dow on January 2, 2004 (Figure 4.9). Second, the last day on the chart makes a slight new high but fails to hold its gains, thus creating a potential upthrust. These are minor changes in behavior and only point to a correction. A swing trader would take profits, while the position trader would keep stops at 30.51. The resulting sell-off bottomed nine sessions later at 33.19. The larger up-move peaked in March 2004, two months after our study ended, at 40.15. A large base formed in U.S. Steel between November 2000 and March 2003. The point-and-figure count made across this base projected a maximum rise to 43.

Drawing from the information already presented about reading bar charts, look at the price rise in October 2012 sugar (Figure 4.14) and make as many observations as you can regarding the lines and the price/volume behavior. They nicely explain what has taken place and build a solid argument for the

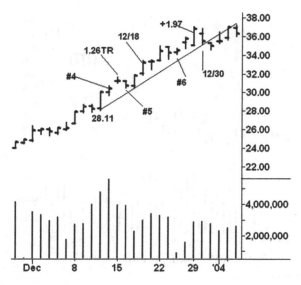

FIGURE 4.13 U.S. Steel Daily Chart 4
Source: TradeStation.

market's future direction. Starting from the liftoff on June 2, I have numbered every fifth day for reference points. The last day shown is number
34. Imagine you are examining this chart after the close on day 34, and you
begin by framing the price movement with horizontal and diagonal lines.
Here are my notes:

1. Horizontal lines are drawn across the highs of day 2 (20.29), 12 (21.14),
   24 (23.05), and 32 (23.99). They depict the shortening of the thrust on
   the successive up-waves. Smaller horizontal lines are drawn across day 3
   and 26 lows. A spring occurs on the small sell-off below day 3.
2. The reverse-trend line comes closest to pinpointing the high; it is drawn
   across the high of day 2 and 21.
3. A parallel line drawn across the low of day 8 creates a reverse-trend
   channel. Note the low on day 30 holds on this line.
4. A second parallel line can be drawn across the low of day 14.
5. As we saw on Figure 4.4, the uptrend was perpetuated because the
   threatening price bars failed to produce greater weakness. In other
   words, lack of downward follow through. The threatening price action
   occurred on day 2, 13, 17, 21, 24, and 26. With the exception of day 26,
   each of these down days was accompanied by heavy volume. With the
   exception of day 2, all of them had wide ranges.

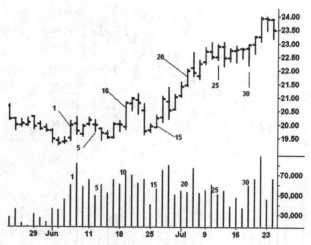

FIGURE 4.14   October 2012 Sugar Daily Chart
Source: TradeStation.

6. The volume on day 32 stands out as the largest on the chart. Its range is the third largest of the up days. It signals climactic behavior.
7. When viewed together, the movement from the bottom of day 30 to the high of day 32 is the steepest three-day rise on the chart (179 points), thus underscoring the climactic action.
8. On day 33, the market tried to turn down but prices recovered to close near the high and only slightly lower. The lack of upward follow-through after day 33 adds to the bearish picture.

At this point, one should have understood the factors that prolonged the up-move from the June low and recognized the market's vulnerability at the close of day 34. The next eight sessions are shown on Figure 4.15. The narrow range on day 35 certainly gave the buyers another chance to take prices higher as the market held on top of day 24. We could not have known the market would have its largest down-bar on the next day, yet it happened. Day 36 is an overtly bearish change in behavior because of its true range, high volume, and weak close. It increases the likelihood of a much larger down-move. Over the next three sessions, however, sugar holds above the line drawn across the low of day 26. An outside, downward reversal occurs on day 39 but the position of the close lessens the bearish message for that session. On day 40, price slips below the support line but recovers to close near the high and only 0.08 points lower. Here, we have a potential spring and

THE LOGIC OF READING BAR CHARTS

once again cannot rule out another attempt to rally. Day 41 is the *coup de grace*: no upward follow-through with the close below the previous day's low. At this point, we know with near certainty that prices are headed lower. The mark-down should begin in earnest. Instead, the range narrows, volume diminishes, and the contract closes a mere four ticks lower on the last day. Imagine you went short on day 34 or 41. Do you believe the last day's action negates the preponderance of bearish behavior that preceded it? Does it warrant closing out the short position? Here, we have one of those moments in the evolution of a trade where we have to be willing to expose ourselves to the unknown. I call it "finding out expense." From the close of day 42, October sugar fell 183 points over the next nine sessions. Each day in this decline had a lower high, low, and close. Each close settled below the low of the preceding day.

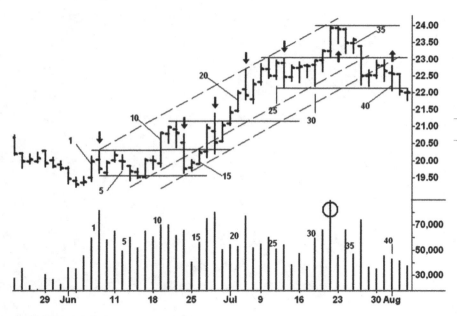

FIGURE 4.15   October 2012 Sugar Chart 2
Source: TradeStation.

From the examples presented in this chapter, you should be better pre-pared to read any bar chart—intraday to monthly—with much greater ease. Instead of analyzing an array of indicators or algorithms, you should be able to listen to what any market says about itself. Such powerful knowl-edge comes from repeatedly observing the story of the lines and the price/volume behavior together.

CHAPTER 5

Springs

When I speak at workshops or traders camps, I introduce the subject of springs and upthrusts with the following statement: **You can make a living by trading springs and upthrusts.** Once you become attuned to the behavior of a spring (and upthrust) your eyes will be opened to an action signal that works in all time periods. The spring can provide the impetus for a short-term pop playable by day traders or serve as the catalyst for long-term capital gains.

For me, a spring is a washout (penetration) of a trading range or support level that fails to follow through and leads to an upward reversal. The duration of the trading range does not have to meet a prescribed amount. My view comes from years of tracking intraday price movement where four days' bond data, for example, represent 320 price bars on a five-minute chart (day session only). A washout of a support level or trading range consisting of 320 price bars suddenly looks like a worthwhile trading situation. The potential gain created by a spring on a five-minute or monthly chart is a function of the underlying trend, market volatility and point and figure preparation. This last statement points to three important concepts regarding springs. First, when a market breaks below a well-defined support line and fails to follow through, I consider it to be in a "*potential* spring position." In other words, the lack of follow-through raises the possibility of an upward reversal or spring. It does not guarantee a spring. As we will see, the price/volume behavior and broader context surrounding the spring situation help determine its probability and significance. Second, springs in an uptrend have a higher percentage of success. Contrarily, if a potential spring in a downtrend fails to develop, short sellers gain useful trading information. Third, a market's volatility often dictates the size of a spring's upward reversal. The amount of preparation, that is, the size of the trading range, can also determine the magnitude of the up-move generated by the spring. Preparation refers to the amount of congestion on a point-and-figure chart that can be used to make price projections.

While Wyckoff did not write about springs per se, he discussed how markets test and retest support levels. These tests give the large operators an opportunity to gauge how much demand exists around well-defined support levels. An engineered sell-off below such support levels provides the ultimate test. If the breakdown fails to produce an onslaught of new selling, the large operator recognizes the supply vacuum and buys aggressively, thus producing fast reversal action. Declines below support levels are often aided by stop-loss selling. As Humphrey Neill wrote in his *Tape Reading and Market Tactics*, markets are "honeycombed with buying and selling orders."[1] Some stop-loss selling offsets long positions, while another portion may be new shorts entering on weakness in expectation of a larger decline. Market moves in reaction to bearish earnings reports or economic data often trigger such stop-loss selling. When prices fall below a support level, I visualize a boxing match. If a boxer knocks his opponent out of the ring and into the fifth row of seats, the opponent should not recover and return to the ring, slugging away with renewed vigor. The breakdown tilts the scales in favor of the sellers. They are supposed to capitalize on their advantage. When this fails to occur, one can go long with a stop below the low of the break. This is buying at the danger point where the risk is smallest; however, it does not mean we automatically buy every breakdown in hope of a reversal. We do not stand in front of onrushing trains and try to pick up loose change.

Since a decline below a trading range raises the possibility of a spring, you may wonder what size sell-off fits the definition of a spring. Unfortunately, no precise rules will work, but guidelines can be helpful. A "relatively small penetration" gives the right look. Such terminology does not convey much meaning; the meaning comes through experience as when we eye a board and say it measures about one foot. In Chapter 3, we discussed a wide-open break (4/4/2000) on the QQQ chart (Figure 3.9). This portion of the chart is enlarged in Figure 5-1, and it concludes with the price action on April 4. Here, the original trading range

---

[1] Humphrey B. Neill, *Tape Reading and Market Tactics* (Burlington, VT: Fraser Publishing, 1970), 188.

between March 10 and 16 spans 15.44 points. The sell-off on April 4 falls 12.69 points below 101.00 or 82 percent of the trading range. If we considered only the size of the break, we would rule out a spring, even though the stock recovered to close above the March 16 low. At the low on April 4, the stock had depreciated 14 percent from the previous day's close and 12.5 percent below the low of the trading range. The magnitude of this sell-off portends much greater weakness ahead. As previously noted, the volume and the price range on April 4 were record levels at that time.

FIGURE 5.1 QQQ Daily Chart
Source: TradeStation.

A few weeks later, QQQ stabilized and a trading range developed between 78 and 94.25 (Figure 5.2). The spring began on May 22 where the stock broke below 78 and reversed upward. At this point, the buyers appeared to overcome the heavy selling; however, the buying evaporated on May 23 and prices reversed downward to close below the trading range and near the day's low. The boxer has been soundly knocked out of the ring and into the fifth row of seats. He is not supposed to recover. Yet, on May 24, the stock reverses upward again and closes on a strong note above the lower boundary of the trading range. The heavy volume and strong close indicate the force of the buying has overcome the force of the selling. At its lowest point, the decline below 78 netted a 7 percent reduction in price. (On

April 4 (Figure 5.1), one might have argued the buyers overcame the selling but the magnitude of the break far exceeded the norm—a Pyrrhic victory for the buyers.)

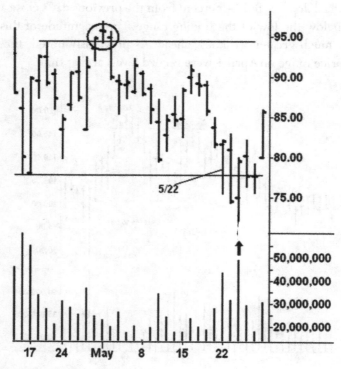

FIGURE 5.2 QQQ Daily Chart 2
Source: TradeStation.

Not all springs occur on heavy volume. There are occasions when prices slip to new lows without a sharp expansion of volume and reverse upward. An example appears on the cocoa daily continuation chart (Figure 5.3) between April and July 2004. On May 18, cocoa broke below the April 21 low at 2196 and fell to 2170. Prices reversed upward on May 18 to close above 2196. The penetration of support required little effort and failed to attract an influx of new selling; therefore, a spring developed. I vividly remember this situation. I did not go long on May 18 and the lack of acceleration on May 19 kept me on the sidelines. On May 20, after the gap opening above the previous day's high, I instantly went long and protected just under the unchanged level. The jump above the previous day's high removed any doubt

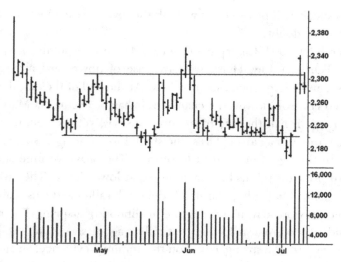

FIGURE 5.3 Cocoa Daily Continuation Chart
Source: TradeStation.

about market direction. This acceleration led to a 175-point rally but no sustained trend. After the rally to the May high, prices returned to the bottom of the trading range. The market made several attempts to lift off, but its inability to rally away from the danger point increased the chances for another breakdown. Notice the poor closings on most of the quick up-moves as the sellers repeatedly thwarted the rallies. The spring from the July low lead to a 450 point rally but to make the trade one would have had to buy quickly.

Many springs cause fast, profitable trades without triggering bigger moves. They give great action signals for 1- to 10-day swings. Figure 5.3 shows a second spring on July 2, where prices dropped to 2158 with a modest increase in volume. Since this decline penetrated the previous low by one point, we could say a minor spring occurred on the test of the earlier spring. Such behavior is not out of the ordinary and sometimes occurs with an even larger penetration on the second spring. Time will tell if the second spring starts a sustained up-move; however, because the sellers again lost their advantage, the odds favor a larger advance. The two breakdowns on this chart fell a tiny percentage below their trading range. One might surmise that the low volume, which reflected a lack of selling pressure, contributed to the small penetration. Sometimes, however, a small breakdown will occur on heavy volume prior to a spring. When this happens, we should take note of the large effort and little reward: it says someone is taking all the supply—especially if price closes well off the low; a weak close would keep the outcome in doubt.

On March 10, 2004, Caterpillar (Figure 5.4) fell 1.38 points (3.6 percent) below its February low. Here, we have ease of downward movement, a weak close, and a large increase in volume. At the end of the day, the sellers have gained control; however, a change in behavior occurs on March 11—the daily range is half the size of the previous day, yet the volume remains about the same. On a closing basis, the stock loses a meager $0.18. We pay attention to the big effort and little reward. The heavy volume and slight downward progress tell us buying emerged at lower levels. They warn of a potential spring. On Friday, March 12, the stock rallies and closes above the high of the previous day, increasing the likelihood of a spring. The narrow-range inside day on March 15 does not reflect aggressive selling; it is a classic secondary test of a spring. Based on this minimal evidence, an aggressive trader might establish a long position on the opening of the next day with a stop below 36.26. Many springs—especially those where the breakdown occurred on heavy volume—are retested. The test of a spring offers an excellent opportunity to go long as it represents higher support. Ideally, the daily range should narrow and the volume taper off on the secondary test of a spring. Yet, no one should depend on exact adherence to the ideal.

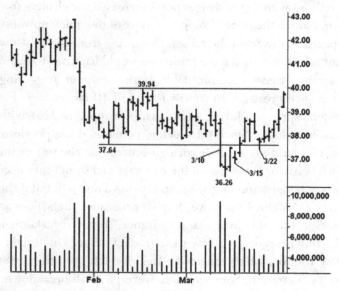

FIGURE 5.4 Caterpillar Daily Chart
Source: TradeStation.

On the Caterpillar chart, another secondary test occurred on March 22. Here, the stock fell below the February support line but recovered to close above it; volume decreased to the lowest reading since the breakdown on March 10. On the QQQ chart (Figure 5.2), the secondary test on Friday, May 26, looks typical with a midrange close slightly above the previous day's close and a distinct drop in volume. One would go long on the next day's opening and protect below the low of May 26. After the secondary tests on the QQQ and Caterpillar charts, prices rose $22 and $4, respectively. Neither of these springs occurred at the bottom of a major decline. The spring in QQQ occurred within the confines of a larger top formation, and the Caterpillar spring developed in the midst of an unresolved top formation. Keep in mind the model of "Where to Find Trades." As previously stated, many trades occur around the edges of trading ranges. Some will lead to prolonged moves; others will be short lived.

When the initial breakdown occurs on heavy volume, the propensity exists for a secondary test. Springs following a low-volume breakdown, like the two on the cocoa chart, are tested less often. But we find plenty of ambiguity regarding springs and secondary tests. Now look at the IBM chart (Figure 5.5). On August 6, 2003, the stock penetrated the bottom of a two-month trading range and reversed to close well above the day's low. It also closed at a price equal to the bottom of the trading range. Thus, the attempted breakdown was a failure. This brief washout occurred with no increase in volume. Prices bobbed back into the trading range and then held in a narrow range between August 11 and 14. Here, the stock displayed a distinct unwillingness to move lower, as indicated by the position of the closes during these four days. This behavior represents a secondary test of the spring in which prices hold at a higher level instead of returning closer to the actual low. The holding action during this secondary test revolved around the high of August 11. As soon as the stock closed above this minor resistance level, price rallied toward the downtrend line before encountering resistance near 85. The upward spike and weak close on Friday, August 22, indicated the stock would sell off again. Notice how the stock found support once more on top of the August 11 high. Between August 26 and 29 (see circled area), the four closings clustered together within a 50-cent range. With the exception of the narrow range on August 27, all of the closes were near the high of each day, indicating the presence of buying at lower levels. The narrow-range inside day on August 29 reflected a total lack of selling pressure. Notice also how the price swings from the May high steadily contracted, with the smallest movement occurring on the decline from the August 22 high. The stock is poised to rally. Wyckoff referred to this as a *springboard*. One can call it another test of the spring or a springboard; the message comes from the price/volume behavior, not the terminology. You only need to know how to read the three basic elements—price range, position of the close, volume—and see them within the context of the lines and the larger time frames.

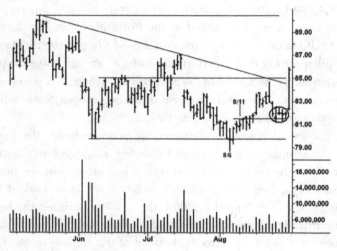

FIGURE 5.5 IBM Daily Chart
Source: TradeStation.

The subject of larger time frames leads me to Union Pacific (Figure 5.6), where a seemingly minor spring occurred in March 2000. The daily chart shows a 10-month decline, where prices stayed within a well-defined down-channel, repeatedly found support around the demand line of the channel, and each important support level served as resistance on later rallies. I have included the low price at each of these support levels, as they reveal behavior that is akin to a spring. If we measure the amount of downward progress from May to February, we see a succession of lows that are 4.66, 3.97, and 1.56 points apart. The stock lost 81 cents on the final decline. Wyckoff referred to this behavior as *shortening of the thrust.* (On charts, I often designate this behavior with the abbreviation SOT; it also occurs on up-moves.) Shortening of the thrust reflects loss of momentum. Whenever the volume becomes heavy at the low points of each down-move and the downward progress diminishes, pay close attention. It means the big effort earned little reward because demand is emerging at

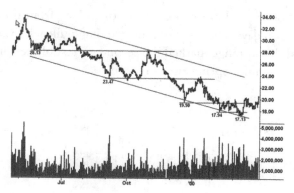

FIGURE 5.6 Union Pacific Daily Chart
Source: TradeStation.

lower levels. If the volume diminishes as the downward thrust shortens, we know the sellers are tiring. These same observations apply to a spring. A penetration of support on heavy volume with only slight downward progress reflects little reward for the effort. A penetration of support on low volume and little downward progress says supply is spent. Regarding the behavior on the Union Pacific chart, we would say March 2000 represents shortening of the downward thrust within the context of the entire decline from the May 1999 low. Within the context of the trading range that began from the February 2000 low at 17.94, the 81-cent drop to the March low is viewed as a spring. In Chapter 3, we observed an apex and spring on the daily Schlumberger chart (Figure 3.12). On its weekly chart (Figure 3.13), the sell-off to the December 1998 low had shortening of the downward thrust. **The main idea behind the notion of springs, upthrusts, and shortening of the thrust is lack of follow-through.** It goes to the heart of the matter.

The details of the spring deserve some attention before we look at the larger context. I have enlarged the Union Pacific trading range (Figure 5.7) from the February low at 17.94. On March 13, the stock fell to 17.13, putting it slightly below the demand line of the down-channel and thus creating a minor oversold condition. The narrowing of the price spread, low volume, and position of the close on this day indicated the selling pressure was at least temporarily spent. On March 14, the stock held in a narrower range and closed fractionally higher; it showed no willingness to return to the previous day's low. The shortening of the downward thrust in an oversold position within the down-channel suggested that a spring could happen. It occurred on March 15–16, where the wide price ranges reflected ease of upward movement. All of the selling from the March high was erased in two days. The low-volume, grinding pullback into the middle of the vertical, liftoff range marked the secondary test of the spring. On the secondary test, a minor spring also occurred.

FIGURE 5.7   Union Pacific Daily Chart (Enlargement)
Source: TradeStation.

SPRINGS

On the monthly Union Pacific chart (Figure 5.8), we see the stock "backed and filled" for another five months between 23 and 18.50 before the trend turned up. But this chart also reveals something quite significant about the minor spring in March 2000. The down-move in March washed out the August 1998 low, creating a spring of much larger degree. Therefore, the six-month trading range between April and September 2000 was a secondary test of this larger spring. Notice the narrowing of the price range in September 2000, the smallest in five years. It said the selling pressure was spent and the stock was on the springboard for a much larger up-move. Attention should also be paid to the price tightness, as it is particularly meaningful when it appears on monthly charts. This observation is most important.

Monthly charts are read in the same manner as daily charts with emphasis on range, position of the close, and volume. Nowhere does this stand out better than on the monthly EWJ chart (Figure 5.9). After declining for two years, this stock found support in February 2002 (point 1). The initial rally met resistance at a previous breakdown point. Prices then fell for five months to the October low (point 2), where support was penetrated and volume soared to 48 million shares. Despite the large effort, the stock closed in midrange and above the February low.

FIGURE 5.8 Union Pacific Monthly Chart
Source: TradeStation.

FIGURE 5.9 Japan Index Fund (EWJ) Monthly Chart
Source: TradeStation.

This suggested a possible spring, but the stock held for four months without any ability to lift away from the danger point. The narrow range, weak close and low volume in February 2003 (point 3) warned of a breakdown. In March and April (points 4 and 5), the stock fell to new lows on heavy volume. Here, we have no ease of downward movement and little reward for the effort; however, the April close provided a clue the stock could rally. The spring began with the turnaround in May. Supply was met in July (point 6), but it was absorbed in August and the stock rallied to 15.55 in May 2006.

Trading ranges lasting many years often contain numerous springs that provide highly profitable, intermediate up-moves without ever producing a major breakout. The soybeans quarterly continuation chart (Figure 5.10) presents a classic example. Without delving too deeply into the many springs on this chart, five stand out. From left to right, they produced gains of $6.36 (16 months), $3.87 (7 months), $6.32 (21 months), $2.31 (9 months), and $6.39 (27 months). A later spring from the 2006 low gained $11.39 in 22 months, and it did represent a major breakout of the trading range shown here. Not bad, considering one dollar in soybeans equals $5,000 per contract. Because of its tendency for multimonth springs, the soybean market is well worth studying closely. Several of these springs were preceded by upward reversals that initially failed to ignite larger moves. The preceding measurements are made from the final starting points. Prior to 1999, all of the springs occurred within the boundary created by the 1975 low and the 1977 high. The 1973 high was not retested until the 2008 rise to 16.63. The trend of commodities peaked in 1980 and did not reach its bottom until 1999, the same year the soybean market broke below its 1975 low. The 1999 low in soybeans was tested several times but continued to hold until the process ended in January 2002. The price action between 1999 and 2002 is a terminal shakeout because it came at the end of a prolonged trading range and evolved over a longer period of time. This kind of price action often will resolve a multiyear trading range and start a much larger uptrend. While much of the rally from the 2002 low was erased in 2004, it ultimately served as a secondary test of the terminal shakeout. On the yearly soybean oil chart (Figure 3.6), we observed a terminal shakeout of the 1975 low. It, too, occurred in the 2001 period and produced a large up-move. On the same yearly chart, the trading range that began from the early 1950s was resolved by a less dramatic terminal shakeout in 1968.

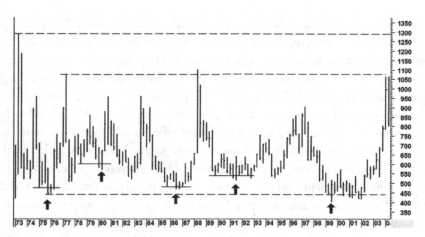

FIGURE 5.10 Soybeans Quarterly Continuation Chart
Source: MetaStock.

The Dow Jones Industrial Average (Figure 5.11) rallied to 1000 for the first time in 1966. From this high, it held for 16 years in a trading range where springs, upthrusts, a terminal shakeout, and an apex developed. The spring in August 1982 was accompanied by the heaviest monthly volume in the history of the stock exchange up to that time. Before August 1982, the daily New York Stock Exchange (NYSE) volume had never reached 100 million shares, and that month it happened on five separate days. The monthly range in August 1982 was the second largest of all previous up months— exceeded only by January 1976. Of course, October 1982 had the largest range for all previous up or down months. To dissect this spring we begin with the break from the 1981 high that found support at 807 in September. From this low, the Dow attempted to recover but ran out of steam above 900 in December. The first quarter of 1982 saw more weakness, plus a new low in March, where we observe three important features: the close ended well off the low of the monthly range, it stood a fraction below the previous month's close, and it recovered above the 1981 low. Together, these three features warned of a potential spring. Monthly NYSE volume in March 1982 reached a historic high, yet the large selling effort netted only a small reward, which added to the bullish picture. A small spring occurred, but it met resistance above 850 in May. The pullback from the May high can be viewed as the test of the spring that developed from the March low. June looked like a successful secondary test of the spring as the Dow held its low and ended the month well off its low. In July, however, the rally sputtered and stopped, as evident by the position of the close. This set the stage for another test of the spring. In August, prices fell to a slight new low. Yet when the Dow recovered intramonth above the July high, the spring was in high gear. The liftoff exceeded the highs of the previous 11 months and heralded the beginning of a once-in-a-lifetime bull market. One might ask why the spring in August 1982 had such a profound effect while the others failed to produce a sustained bull move. One obvious, nontechnical reason has to do with interest rates. Long-term yields peaked in September 1981, and short-term yields fell sharply in August 1982. From a purely technical standpoint, the coiling of prices into an apex helped unleash such a powerful rally on the spring. Also, some of the longer-term price cycles bottomed in 1982. The tediousness of the turnaround from the 1982 low testifies to the stock market's uncanny ability to prolong a trend. We have seen the same kind of behavior throughout the 2011–2012 period. The subject of upthrusts will be dealt with in the next chapter but Figure 5.11 provides several excellent examples.

As we have seen, springs in long-term, volatile trading ranges such as shown on the Dow and soybean charts often provide major buying

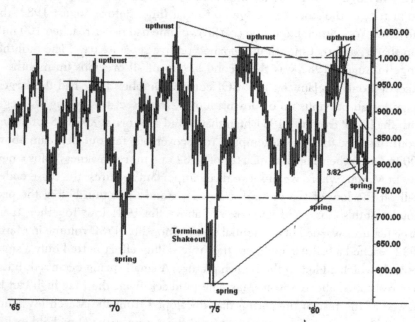

FIGURE 5.11 Dow Jones Industrial Average Monthly Chart
Source: TradeStation.

opportunities. Within daily uptrends, springs sometimes occur at the right-hand side of corrections. They can be used to pyramid long positions or get aboard after a trend has begun. Downtrends are littered with failed springs (see Figure 5.6). They create what I call a *bottom picker's nightmare,* as they repeatedly entice traders to chase upward reversals. These are usually short lived and, when read correctly, can be used for establishing short positions. We will look first at two uptrends starting with the daily chart of Deere & Co. (Figure 5.12) between March and October 2003. The stock market made an important low in March 2003 that produced an orderly uptrend for about one year. On the daily charts of the S&P and other indices/averages, the reversal action at the March low was quite obvious. Deere followed the herd but without giving any overt indications prior to its liftoff. In other words, there was no climactic volume, no shortening of the downward thrust, no reversal action, and no oversold condition within the down-channels from the December 2002 high. On the weekly chart (not shown), the decline from December 2002 to March 2003 did retest the July 2002 low. But nothing occurred from a price/volume perspective that pointed to the start of a large up-move. Yet the stock rallied briskly off its low to the March 21 high in concert with the broader market. Then the stock gave back most of its gains on the next correction. From this low, the stock gradually rose to the 22 level, where the heavy volume on May 12–13 indicated the presence of supply. A trading range formed for a few weeks prior to the minor breakdown on May 29. Volume rose to the highest level in 11 days, and price closed near the low of the day. The lack of downward follow-through on the next day put the stock in a potential spring position. (It also increased the likelihood that the stock had been undergoing absorption around the level of the March high.) One could go long on May 30 or June 2 with a stop below the May 29 low. Even though the volume increased on the breakdown, no secondary test occurred. Making small bets on minor springs of this sort has a greater chance of success in an uptrend. The second spring resolved the trading range between the June high and July low. On July 16, the stock fell below the trading range and closed on a weak note; volume remained low.

One of my favorite kinds of springs occurred on the 17th. Here, the stock gapped higher—almost to the previous day's high—and volume soared. This kind of spring action rarely works in a downtrend; in an uptrend, however, it reinforces the bullish story, as it makes would-be buyers pay up to own the stock and prevents others from getting aboard. On this spring, we have a low-volume break, followed by high volume on the up day and the next day's secondary test. Then the stock quickly rose above the June high. Notice the pullback in early August that tested the breakout where demand overcame supply, as depicted in Figure 1.1. Price accelerated upward in August, and ultimately became mired in another trading range. On September 26, the stock fell below the lower boundary of this range without any increase in volume. (It tested the vertical acceleration of August 12.) The lack of volume and follow-through on the next day raised the possibility of a spring. I like to see such buoyant behavior. A narrow-range inside day (9/29) holding just below the low of the range demands an immediate rally or lookout below. In a downtrend, there would be little doubt of the outcome. Here, the underlying trend sweeps away all doubt as the stock rallies away from the danger point. The low volume on the September spring has added significance in that it tested the vertical, high-volume area of August 12–13. The low volume reflected a lack of supply in an area where demand had previously overcome supply. Evidently, few trapped shorts were enticed to increase their position on the September 26 breakdown. The stock reached 37.47 in April 2004.

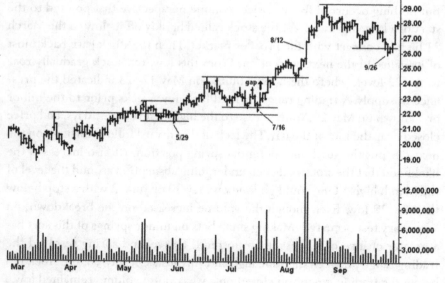

FIGURE 5.12 Deere & Co. Daily Chart
Source: TradeStation.

The uptrend in the December 2004 Eurodollar chart (Figure 5.13) between November 2003 and March 2004 contains numerous springs and tests of high-volume breakout areas. The chart offers an exceptional study of the "story of the lines." For background information, this contract peaked in June 2003 at 98.39 and declined to the August 2003 low at 96.87.

After consolidating for one month, prices rose sharply on September 4–5. This vertical liftoff provided the impetus for the rally to the October high, where the chart shown here begins. Quite naturally, the correction from the October high tested the area where prices rose vertically in early September. This correction is labeled as trading range AB. From the October low, a smaller trading range, BC, developed. Its first high point ended slightly within the daily range of October 3, where prices accelerated lower on increased volume. The high-volume sell-off on November 7 broke below ranges AB and BC, but the position of the close and the lack of reward for the effort suggested that a spring would occur. When the contract pressed upward two days later, one should have gone long with a stop below the immediate low. This spring accelerates upward on November 13–14 before petering out on Monday the 17th. On the latter day, the narrowing of the price range said the spring was losing momentum Of course, this was again in the area of the October 3 breakdown and also created a potential upthrust of trading range BC. An active trader might have taken profits or made a bigger bet by holding for the secondary test. The upthrust was not completed until November 21 and led to a test of the spring. On December 5, after the retest of the low, the contract rose sharply on heavy volume, erasing most of the previous down-move. The ease of upward movement, strong close, and high volume augured for further price gains. Prices first experienced a choppy holding action, as the buyers absorbed through the remaining supply before the breakout on December 11. The breakout was short lived as the contract met resistance on the next day. A new trading range, DE, formed essentially on top of BC and mostly within the price range of the December 11–12 breakout. In the context of the drawing shown in "Where to Find Trades," trading range DE is a more drawn-out test of the breakout. Its resolution occurs with the spring on January 2. While the contract broke with ease on Friday, January 2, the minuscule volume suggested a washout of weak longs rather than supply overcoming demand. The low volume and narrow range on the next day underscored the lack of supply and provided an excellent place to go long (or even on the following day's opening for traders who use end-of-day data). In the next three sessions (see circled area), the market holds tightly against the resistance line as the buyers absorb through the overhead supply.

For traders who saw how the closes on these three days were clustered together and well above their respective intraday lows, the absorption area offered an excellent place to establish longs. On January 9, demand overcomes supply as prices move upward with great ease and force. The rally promptly stops on the next day; prices seemingly consolidate on top of resistance line A and then push upward to another high (1/23). We immediately notice how the thrust shortened on the rally above the previous high (1/10) and prices reversed lower. Suddenly, we are faced with the possibility that the latest breakout has produced an upthrust of trading range AB. The swing trader takes profits; the active trader makes a bet on the short side, with a stop immediately above January 23. The potential upthrust becomes more plausible after the high-volume, wide-open break on January 28. While this decline has tested the breakout and held on top of resistance line D, the weak close and large volume favor further weakness. It is the action on January 29 that reduces bearish expectations. Here, the daily range narrows, prices close in midrange, and volume soars to the highest reading on the chart as the market returns to the previous absorption area. Some large interests were obviously buying in the face of heavy selling; thus, the contract made little downward progress. The swing trader might reestablish long positions with a stop slightly below 97.80 (the absorption area); anyone determined to stay short should at least adjust stops to break even. We now have a new trading range, FG, interacting with the tops of AB and DE. Support line G is almost an extension of resistance line D. On the subsequent rally, the narrowing of the daily ranges above 98.00 indicates demand is tiring. This leads to a pullback on February 6 to test the January 28 low. But the contract reverses upward with great force locking out anyone waiting for a spring.

I began this chapter by saying how one can make a living trading springs and upthrusts. Statistically speaking, springs and upthrusts are not as prevalent as double tops and bottoms. Look through a chart book and you will find plenty of six-month or one-year uptrends without any springs. Yet trading strategies for handling these situations can be made. One strategy involves going long on the pullback after the high-volume rally off a low. Many times there are shallow corrections into the range of the high-volume day(s)—such as after December 5, January 2, and February 6 in this study—that can be used for buying. Of course, other trades can be established in absorption areas or on tests of breakouts. After February 6, the contract experiences another sharp run-up on the 11th. Volume remains heavy and provides enough force to break out of trading range FG. As occurred after the December 11 and January 9 rallies, the ranges narrow as upward momentum tires. On February 18, however, the contract reverses to close near the day's low, raising the possibility that trading range FG has been upthrusted. We see the shortening of the upward progress as measured from the highs of line D, F, and H. Yet, the ensuing correction, labeled trading range HJ, is shallow. It tests and holds within the vertical range of February 11 and ends with an almost imperceptible spring on March 3. The spring consists of a narrow range with a firm close above the bottom of the trading range. Huge demand appears on March 5 as the contract races to a new high. In retrospect, trading range HJ represents absorption around the top of trading range FG and on top of AB.

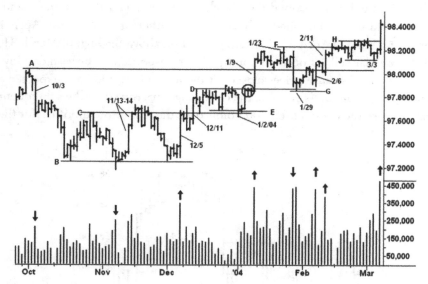

FIGURE 5.13 December 2004 Eurodollar Daily Chart
Source: TradeStation.

The uptrend shown here has responded to one spring after another with great ease of upward movement and increased volume. Because of the heavy volume, each spring quickly dissipated, leading to another trading range. This has not been a steady, grinding uptrend with the buyers in complete control—a more bullish condition. High volume throughout an uptrend reflects the presence of persistent selling that has to be absorbed before the trend continues. After the high-volume breakout on March 5, a small trading range, KL, formed on Figure 5.14. It ended with a tiny spring on March 16. Compare the character of the rally on this spring with the earlier reversals on Figure 5.12. Suddenly, the daily ranges narrow and volume diminishes, indicating a lack of demand. The drying up of demand at the top of the March 2004 rally becomes more ominous when one considers that the move has barely exceeded the June 2003 high at 98.39. The topping action is worth discussing. Notice the weak position of the close on the top day (3/24) and how much of the spring was erased two days later. Yet on March 31, the contract still had another opportunity to recover after the buyers did not allow further weakness and prices closed on a strong note. At this point, the market was in a position similar to December 4, January 5, and March 4. Instead, on April 1, there was no follow-through buying and prices reversed to close at the low of the previous three sessions. The sellers had absorbed the buying around the March 16 low and gained the upper hand. One could have established a short position either on the close of April 1 or the opening of April 2, with stop protection above the high of March 31. A spectacular sell-off occurred on April 2 in response to a bearish employment report. Because prices closed off the low, one would have expected a knee-jerk rebound. As you see, the daily ranges narrowed on the subsequent rally before the contract fell 100 points over the next three months. But the

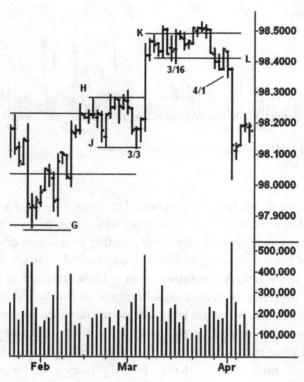

FIGURE 5.14 December 2004 Eurodollar Chart 2
Source: TradeStation.

failed spring on March 31–April 1 created the immediate, technical setup for lower prices; the shortening of the upward thrust in March and the upthrust of the June 2003 high painted a much larger bearish picture; the overtly bearish fundamentals provided the reason. Now we'll examine failed springs in a top formation.

The cotton market doubled in price between October 2001 and October 2003. The new-crop December 2004 contract (Figure 5.15) peaked at 71 cents and experienced a fast sell-off to 62.50 in November 2003. From this low, the contract rebounded to 69.96 in January 2004 where our study begins. The daily chart shows the top formation that developed between January and April 2004. It is marked by a number of failed springs, which underscored the growing strength of the sellers. Rather than give a blow-by-blow account of the action, I am touching on the main points. The springs on February 10 and March 9 throw prices back to the top of trading range AB. But the spring from the low of April 13 only retests the lower line of the trading range. From this last high, the downtrend accelerates on April 28–29. The close on April 29 holds out the chance for a rebound, but it cannot penetrate the downtrend line and more weakness follows. The sell-off on April 29 is too deep to consider a spring. We have on this chart a series of

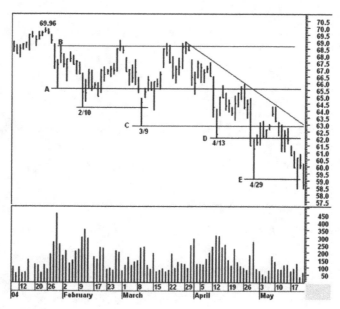

FIGURE 5.15   December 2004 Cotton Daily Chart
Source: TradeStation.

lower lows and highs revolving around axis lines A and C. The holding action at the right edge of the chart is part of an area where the sellers absorbed all buying and prices continued lower.

I know of no better trading strategy than the spring. It produces short-term intraday trades and ignites many long-term trends. For risk management, it offers a way to enter a trade at the danger point where the outcome will be quickly determined and the risk is minimal. When prices move below a line of support, many traders back away for fear of greater weakness. The professional trader knows better. He watches for hesitation or little follow-through and quickly takes advantage of the situation. An understanding of the spring allows anyone to trade like a professional. And it will earn a nice yearly income.

CHAPTER 6

Upthrusts

When a stock, index, or commodity moves above a previous line of resistance and fails to follow through, one has to consider the potential for a downward reversal. Such a failed breakout is called an *upthrust*. Like a spring, it can occur in several ways and it may be retested at a later point. Like a spring, it offers a trading opportunity at the danger point where the risk is the least. It similarly can provide a very fast trading turn within a trend or appear at a major top. I find upthrusts to be more difficult to trade than springs. One reason may be the public's willingness to buy new highs. They are not as anxious to go short on new lows. Thus, we often can discern the professional buying more clearly on a spring. Professional selling at a top may be obscured under cover of the public buying—that's the preferred environment for the professional trader who is working out of a long position and establishing shorts.

Because of the potential for an upthrust, I am not eager to buy breakouts. Jesse Livermore, in his book *How to Trade in Stocks*, expressed the opposite view:

> It may surprise many to know that in my method of trading, when I see by my records that an upward trend is in progress, I become a buyer as soon as a stock makes a new high on its movement, after having had a normal reaction.[1]

Buying new highs is one of the mainstays of the *Investor's Business Daily* trading philosophy. It works extremely well in a bull market. In his excellent book, *How to Make Money in Stocks*, William O'Neil wrote: "The hard to

---

[1] Jesse L. Livermore, *How to Trade in Stocks* (New York: Duell, Sloan, Pearce, 1940), 20.

accept great paradox in the stock market is that what seems high and risky to the majority usually goes higher and what seems low and cheap usually goes lower."[2]

It takes a long time to believe this wise advice. Along the same line, I might add that the popular strategy of being a contrarian in the face of an established trend (up or down) can have disastrous results. So how do we know if a breakout above resistance will fail? The trend is the most important consideration. As will be shown in this chapter, supposed upthrusts in an uptrend rarely pan out. In a downtrend, however, upthrusts above a previous correction high have a greater probability of working. They flourish.

There are almost an infinite number of ways an upthrust can occur. The first prerequisite is a previous high across which a resistance line is drawn. A move above that line becomes a "potential" upthrust. The rise above a previous high may not be the deciding price action. It's often the cumulative behavior on the preceding price bars and especially the succeeding price bars that tell the story. Upthrusts can occur on any chart regardless of the time period. When a market trades at record highs, the volatility usually becomes greater than in many months. In such an environment, an upthrust on an hourly chart can produce a down-move larger than the previous year's range. I am thinking here of silver prices in 2011. Generally speaking, the upthrusts on weekly charts stand out most clearly. Figure 6.1 shows the March–April 2011 top on the weekly chart of Silver Wheaton. A bearish change in behavior occurred in the week ending March 11, where prices fell 7.74 points from high to low. This was the largest down week in the stock's history. Four weeks later (April 8) the stock rallied to close above the March 11 high. The buyers seemingly had regained the upper hand. Yet by the close of the next week, April 15, the stock had reversed downward. At this point, the cumulative behavior indicated an upthrust had occurred.

For the record, Figure 6.2 shows the daily chart of Silver Wheaton. Here, the heavy selling in the March 11 week does not stand out. On the "break-out" day, April 8, the narrowing of the range and the position of the close certainly would have raised suspicions about a potential upthrust. A narrow-range breakout does not speak of aggressive demand capable of resuming an uptrend. But it's the high-volume sell-offs in the next two sessions, April 11 and 12, that prove the sellers have taken control. Figure 6.2 embodies several characteristics of an upthrust. First, the close on April 11 is below the low of April 8 and April 7. Thus, it totally erases the "breakout." Second, it

[2] William J. O'Neil, *How to Make Money in Stocks* (New York: McGraw-Hill, 1995), 25.

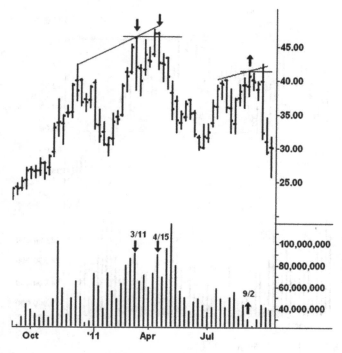

FIGURE 6.1   Silver Wheaton Weekly Chart
Source: TradeStation.

is an unusually large down-bar. The true range on April 11 is the largest for any down-bar since November 10, 2010, almost exactly six months earlier. After the temporary low on April 12, notice how prices flailed up and down and repeatedly closed near the low end of the price bars.

On January 3, 2011, U.S. Steel (Figure 6.3) reached the high point (61.18) of a five-month rally. After a sharp correction, the stock began another up-wave. The gap upward on February 15 exceeded the January high. Although the stock closed near the lower end of its range, the true range gives the close a stronger pallor. Volume increased appropriately and the buyers seemed to have overcome the selling. The range narrowed on the next day as the stock made little upward progress, but the firm close still held open the possibility prices might be levitating higher. More narrowing of the range occurred on February 17, but the firm close and outside upward reversal kept the bullish story alive. We can make endless excuses for this weak rally, but it needs to make greater progress. Instead, the outside, downward reversal on February 18 is a bearish change in behavior. It offers an excellent

FIGURE 6.2 Silver Wheaton Daily Chart
Source: TradeStation.

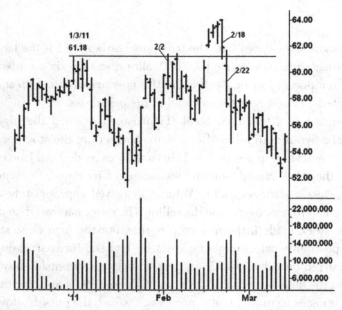

FIGURE 6.3 U.S. Steel Daily Chart
Source: TradeStation.

shorting opportunity with stop placement immediately above the previous day's high. While the volume does not expand sharply, the close below the lows of the previous four sessions is sufficient evidence to say an upthrust has occurred. The wide-open decline on Tuesday, February 22, triples the odds for lower prices. It will be many years before the high of this day is exceeded. Notice the price action on February 2. Here, the stock barely penetrated its January high and reversed lower. Two days later, the same bearish price action occurred. When working with a stock priced at $60, I rarely consider an 18-cent new high to be an upthrust. It's a secondary test or, perhaps, a double top. A fractional new high on a $2 stock could be an upthrust. Overall, there is no precise size measurement for an upthrust to fulfill. A new high by 10 to 15 percent seems a reasonable limitation for an upthrust. Gold futures peaked in March 2008 at 1040. In December 2009 they reversed downward from 1240. This was not an upthrust of the 2008 high. It was the top of a rally within the uptrend.

The Standard & Poor's (S&P) is notorious for its springs and upthrusts. Many of its major extremities were resolved by these two kinds of behavior. Its 60-month advance from the October 2002 low was littered with upthrusts. They produced either short-lived declines or lateral movement but no serious downturn. Eight "potential" upthrusts can be identified on the Cash S&P monthly chart (Figure 6.4). Among these, five were outside downward reversals. Numbers 1, 4, and 8 were the exceptions. The average sell-off on the first six upthrusts was 88 points. With the exception of the correction from the high of number 2, the down-moves never lasted more than three days. I was writing a nightly S&P report during this uptrend, and I'm sure that I mentioned the bearish implications for each one of these reversals. Although they garnered some healthy profits, their longer-term implications were nil. The seventh upthrust in July 2007 looked like the big kahuna. It spawned a 155-point decline and drew out massive selling. Yet in October 2007, the S&P managed to make one final new high, and this time by a mere 21 points. An outside downward reversal occurred on October 11, the top day. This high was also a 24-point upthrust of the 2000 high, which made it more significant. It led to the severe down-move to the 2009 low.

Both of the 2007 upthrusts are shown in greater detail on the weekly continuation chart of S&P futures (Figure 6.5). Upthrust 7 occurred during the week of July 20, 2007. Here, the preceding month's high stands out more clearly. But it's the huge outpouring of supply on the sell-off from the July high that dominates the chart. At that time, it was the heaviest volume in the history of the futures contract. Remember, the heavy volume on the Silver

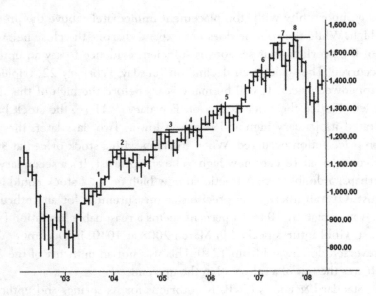

FIGURE 6.4 Cash S&P 500 Monthly Chart
Source: TradeStation.

Wheaton (Figure 6.1) chart gave a similar bearish warning in early March 2011 prior to its upthrust; however, its magnitude was considerably smaller than in the S&P. The four-week sell-off from the July 2007 high netted 192 points. On upthrust number 8, the range narrowed and prices closed well off the high. These narrow-range breakouts should always be eyed suspiciously. Around the 1,500 line the rally attempts were repeatedly blocked as the sellers had gained control.

From the October 2007 upthrust high, S&P futures fell 921 points to the March 2009 low. This 58 percent decline would seem enough to bury the market, but as of this writing it has returned to within 120 points of the 2007 high. We can tell from this recovery and many others of even greater magnitude that an upthrust does not necessarily mean a permanent high has been reached. *Permanence*, like *absolute*, is a word avoided in regard to markets. An upthrust represents ending action but not necessarily terminal action. Look at the copper monthly (Figure 6.6). Its upthrust in 2008, above the 2006 high, looked like the end of a long-term uptrend. Copper prices fell 66 percent in seven months. In February 2011, copper rallied to the top of its up-channel and exceeded its previous high. Notice the clustering of closes between December 2010 and February 2011. On a net basis, this revealed the market's inability to move higher. The upthrust was

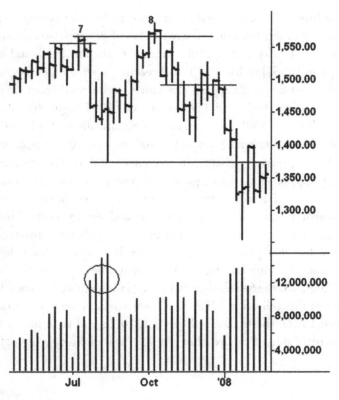

FIGURE 6.5 S&P Continuation Weekly Chart
Source: TradeStation.

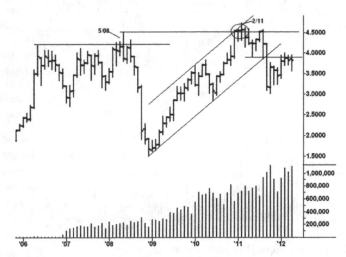

FIGURE 6.6 NY Copper Continuation Monthly Chart
Source: TradeStation.

retested in July 2011, and record selling emerged on the August–September down-move. Many other commodity markets have experienced such wide swings after upthrusts. Cotton, for example, peaked in 1980, and upthrusted this high in 1995, but by 2011 it had reached a price twice as great as the 1995 peak. Anything can happen. The yearly soybean oil chart (Figure 3.6) shows upthrusts in 1974 and 1984 above the 1947 high. Prices exploded above these highs in 2008 and then more dramatically in 2011 and 2012.

Nowhere does the transitory nature of the upthrust appear more frequently than on intraday charts. In this environment, the upthrust, along with the spring, gives traders a great, low-risk edge. Chapter 3 dealt with the importance of framing trading ranges with support and resistance lines. It is around these lines that upthrusts and springs occur. They do not always depend on great volatility. Many times, an upthrust consists of a single five-minute bar that penetrates a resistance line and reverses downward. Nothing could be simpler. Figure 6.7 exemplifies this trading situation. Here, on August 5, the September 2011 S&P falls from a presession high. The initial low of this sell-off is 1202.75. This price later serves as an axis line. Just before 13:00, the market rallies to 1210.25 and then forms a trading range on either side of the axis line. At 13:55, a slight new high (1212.50)

FIGURE 6.7   September 2011 S&P Five-Minute Chart
Source: TradeStation.

is made and the market fails to follow through. In this situation, there is no heavy burst of volume signifying that the sellers have gained the upper hand. Instead, prices have a small reaction at first. A secondary test occurs at 14:40, and the low volume says demand is spent. Trades established on the reversal from the 13:55 high or on the secondary test (1205.75) were rewarded handsomely. Such small upthrusts appear every day. This reversal had a high probability of success because it tested the point on the chart where prices previously broke down. Furthermore, the low volume leading up to the upthrust did not reflect aggressive buying. It looked more like a stop hunt than the beginning of a sustained up-move.

Figure 6.8 (S&P five-minute chart) tells a different story. The increased volume on the breakout bar looks constructive; however, the narrowing of the range and the position of the close override the bullish interpretation. In this context, the increased volume reflects a large effort with a small reward. The outside, downward reversal 10 minutes later adds to the bearish picture. But the price bars narrow on the retest of the support line and show

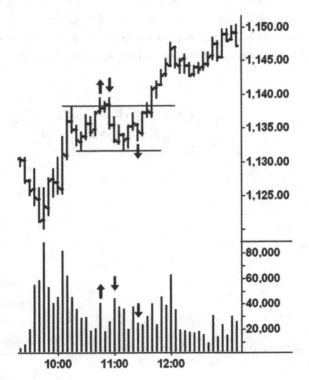

FIGURE 6.8 September 2011 S&P Five-Minute Bar Chart
Source: TradeStation.

the selling pressure is not gathering steam. The last down-bar at 11:25 a.m. holds above the low, does not attract heavy selling, and closes in mid-range. All in all, this is not bearish behavior. Prudence says to close out any short trade. Because of the market's volatility on this day, a quick profit could have been made on what turned out to be a false upthrust. The underlying bullish trend was too strong to allow a larger downturn. As long as the risk is reasonable, however, a nimble day trader can earn a living by probing such potential upthrusts.

In a top formation, there may be several upthrusts before the markdown begins. Figure 6.9 shows an intermediate top in Freeport-McMoran during April 2011. A trading range formed between the first hour's high and the second hour's low on April 25. This narrow range contained most of the price action over the next five trading sessions. As occurs with so many stocks, the heaviest volume normally appears in the first hour. When the heaviest hourly volume occurs in a later period, it is worth noting. I like to denote such aberrations in the pattern of hourly volume with a double arrow. On April 26, the stock makes a slight new high, but the narrowing of the hourly ranges and relatively low volume warn against being too bullish. A better attempt to break out occurs on April 28. Here, the stock closes at its highest price and looks capable of making further gains. By the end of the

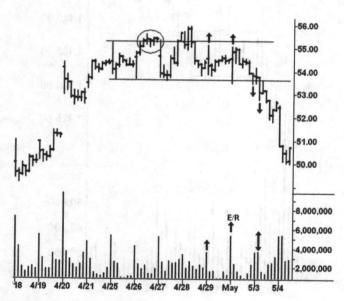

FIGURE 6.9   Freeport-McMoran Hourly Chart
Source: TradeStation.

day, however, the gains are swept away. The effort to move up on April 29 fails to attract follow-through buying. The heaviest up-volume within the trading range occurs in the first hour on May 2, a failed spring. Here is an example of a large effort with no reward (E/R). Taken together, these two surges can be viewed as secondary tests of the April 28 upthrust. Notice how the stock weakens in the last hour on May 2 and closes ominously at the low of the trading range. The volume in the second hour on May 3 exceeds the first hour's volume and shifts the down-move into gear. It bottomed at 46.06 on May 17.

In summary, the trend is of paramount concern when evaluating up-thrusts. It's the price/volume behavior on the preceding and succeeding bars that often reveal if a potential upthrust will actually develop. Upthrusts on weekly and monthly charts usually lead to larger downtrends than those on daily charts. On daily charts, the upthrusts at the tops of rallies may only produce a correction. Finally, more than one upthrust can occur in a top formation before the markdown gets under way. When a market continues to hold against a resistance level and refuses to turn down after several instances of threatening price action, one has to consider absorption is taking place. It is the subject of the next chapter.

CHAPTER 7

Absorption

How do we know if a test or penetration of a high will lead to a break-out or a downward reversal? This is the dilemma we are constantly faced with: take profits or stay long and make ourselves vulnerable to giving back profits. The answer partly depends on one's trading style. A short-term trader, eager to book a profit, will not subject himself to any further un-knowns. A position trader, guided by a longer-term outlook, may choose to endure a correction. Traders who went long at the current price several weeks or even months earlier will usually opt to liquidate positions. They've had enough. Longs who bought at lower levels take profits. Short sellers smell a possible top and put added pressure on the market. Absorption is the process through which the long liquidation, profit taking, and new short selling are overcome. It can show up on any chart, regardless of the time frame.

These clues point to a successful absorption of overhead selling:

- Rising supports.

- Volume increases around the top of the absorption area.

- Lack of downward follow-through after a threatening price bar.

- At the right-hand side of an absorption area, prices tend to press against the resistance line without giving ground.

- In some instances, the absorption phase is resolved by a spring.

- Minor up-thrusts during absorption fail to produce a breakdown.

When viewed as a correction, absorption areas are generally shallow. They often form in the area where prices recently accelerated higher and/or where volume rose sharply.

In Figure 1.1, Where to Find Trades, absorption is shown at the top of the trading range. It most commonly occurs at this location on a chart. But absorption can occur at the bottom of a trading range as the sellers overcome buying. At lows, the buying stems from short covering, short liquidation, and bottom picking by new longs. The main characteristic of sellers overcoming buyers is the repeated inability of prices to rally away from the danger point. Such hugging of the low usually leads to a breakdown. Persistently heavy volume hammering against the low usually says a break is imminent. When the persistent selling against a low fails to produce further weakness, Wyckoff referred to such behavior as "bag-holding." In this situation, the large operators are trapping the shorts. Absorption by sellers is made more difficult to read because some of the rally attempts look like potential springs—but they either fail or are short lived. Absorption does not always take the form of lateral movement. There are occasions when prices simply levitate higher. In these instances, prices climb the proverbial "wall of worry," lock out would-be buyers waiting for a correction, and feed on anyone daring to go short. I think of the Greek phalanx marching in step across the Plain of Troy. Volatility usually stays low until a high-volume wide-range price bar temporarily stops the move. With that said, we will look at various examples of absorption plus some examples where it was negated.

On the whole, most absorption areas continue only a few days or weeks. Absorption on monthly charts can persist much longer. When we frame a trading range with support and resistance lines, the relatively tight absorption areas will stand out. Those contained within a few price bars remind me of a fist. In Figure 7.1, Immersion Corporation churned in a narrow range for four days during June 2007 and then continued higher. Over the next 11 sessions, IMMR appreciated 50 percent.

Looking at the first day of absorption (see arrow), volume soared as the stock reversed to close on a weak note, making the day look most threatening. It raised the specter of an upthrust. Over the next two sessions, prices tried to rally but succumbed to close near their lows. The poor closes and low volumes were not encouraging; however, the lack of downward follow-through after the reversal day said the sellers had so far not capitalized on their advantage. One had to wonder why the market was holding up so well in the face of an "easy" shorting opportunity. On the last day, the stock penetrated the lows of the previous two bars and reversed to close at its highest level to date. This outside, upward reversal was the day to go long and place a protective stop below its low.

I can't help pointing out some of the other behavior on the chart. The trading range in the lower left portion of the chart has a nice spring followed by three inside days on low volume. Do you recognize the behavior circled at the top of this trading range? It can be viewed as absorption or as a pullback to test the breakout. I prefer the latter. The normal up-channel is self-explanatory; its supply line served as resistance twice. The three successive highs at points 1, 2, and 3 illustrate the shortening of the upward thrust.

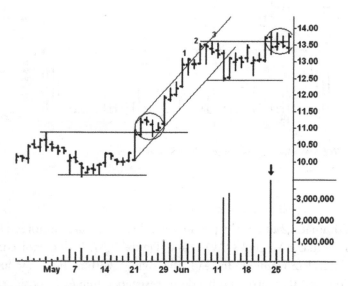

FIGURE 7.1 Immersion Corp. Daily Chart
Source: TradeStation.

In the original Wyckoff course (1931), absorption is first mentioned in his discussion of the *New York Times* average of 50 stocks (Figure 7.2) between the years 1930 and 1931. Wyckoff viewed the 13-day trading range against the January 1931 high as absorption. In that situation the action consisted of rising supports, but price never exceeded the January high until the breakout at the right-hand side. Besides the rising supports, we see two threatening price bars that failed to entice follow-through selling. In the last four days, the closes are clustered in a one-point range. All four closes settle between the high and midpoint of their respective ranges. The pressing against the resistance line leads to the breakout. Many students of Wyckoff's course consider the analysis of this chart to be one of his finest writings. I learned a great deal from this study.

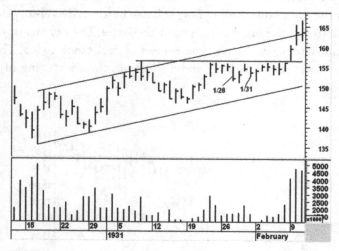

FIGURE 7.2   *New York Times* Average of 50 Stocks Daily
Source: MetaStock.

A less dramatic, but equally productive, absorption area unfolded in April 2009 on the daily Mechel OAO chart (Figure 7.3). It does not consist of narrow, lateral movement. Instead, the swings within the range are relatively wide, and they cross both side of resistance line A. I consider this to be absorption because the trading range worked back and forth across the March high. The rally from the early April low exceeded the February high and reached the top of a minor up-channel, where the thrust shortened. Notice how the correction from the high tested the vertical area where prices accelerated upward. Support formed along line D and slightly above resistance line B. Volumes remained about equal throughout the range, with the exception of the April 30 downward reversal. On this day, the down-volume rose to the highest level since the February high. The stock closed in a vulnerable position but failed to follow through on the next day. Here we have an example of bag-holding. This immediately created a potential spring worthy of buying with a close stop below the low of the previous day. From this point, the stock rose to 12.69 on June 1.

FIGURE 7.3 Mechel OAO Daily
Source: TradeStation.

As mentioned above, what looks like an upthrust can also be part of an absorption area. Figure 7.4 of the June 2012 S&P on April 25, 2012, shows repeated attacks against the morning high that I like to compare to a battering ram at the castle door. While there is little upward follow-through on these thrusts, each pullback holds at a higher level as the buyers steadily push through the overhead supply. The pullbacks after each thrust become shallower and shallower as prices press upward. They give the best clue that prices will move higher. This chart demonstrates why one cannot automatically consider going short when prices fail to immediately follow through after breakouts. It underscores why chart reading is an art rather than a science built on black and white signals.

Distinguishing between an upthrust and absorption sometimes requires paying attention to subtle clues. In Figure 7.5, we see a daily S&P continuation chart where prices move above the September 2009 high and stop. Seven days of lateral movement follow, and they hold on top of the September high. It's not an easy situation to solve. In Chapter 4, I described how uptrends contain numerous threatening price bars that fail to produce greater weakness. We see the same behavior here. Moving from left to right, the first arrow was preceded by an outside downward reversal. Instead of

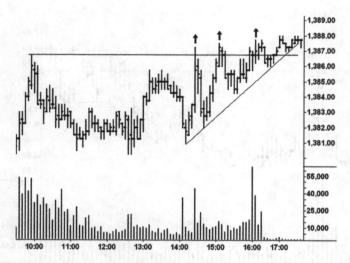

FIGURE 7.4 June 2012 S&P Five-Minute Chart
Source: TradeStation.

FIGURE 7.5 S&P Continuation Daily Chart
Source: TradeStation.

following through on the downside, the market reverses to close on a strong note. But then, once more, the market reverses and closes near the day's low. The third arrow points to another resurgence of buying, and the market has its best chance to move higher. Yet all of the gains made on this day are erased on the next. The volumes on the two down days are the heaviest in the range, which adds weight to the view that an upthrust has occurred. It was the market's inability to take advantage of its two recoveries that led to a 60-point sell-off.

A small trading area around the lower boundary of a larger range often consists of numerous attempts to spring. When these springs repeatedly fail, it is fair to say the sellers are absorbing the buying. They inevitably trap traders who automatically buy any attempt to reverse upward. From its June 2008 high, U.S. Steel (Figure 7.6) fell over $60 in about 20 days. After a fast rebound off the July low, support line B, the downward thrust shortened on the sell-off to the August low (C). This indicated that the downward momentum was tiring. A smaller trading range formed around this low; it consisted of three attempts to spring. The third spring began after a slight penetration of the early August low. There was no strong burst of demand off the low. Prices simply floated upward with small volume and narrow ranges. A short position was warranted once prices gapped lower on the following day's opening. From this point, the stock fell $90 over the next few months.

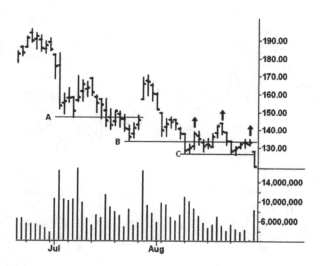

FIGURE 7.6 U.S. Steel Daily
Source: TradeStation.

Absorption by sellers can also be detected when prices are unable to rally away from the lower boundary of a trading range. Instead, they hug the low, and all attempts to lift off are blocked. Sometimes, this kind of price action will last for several weeks. It also occurs frequently on intraday charts. Imagine a situation opposite what we saw in Figure 7.2; when the support finally crumbles, expect a sharp sell-off. Subsequent rallies to test this breakdown often provide excellent shorting opportunities. In Chapter 1, I included the test of a breakdown among the best places to find trades.

Figure 7.7 shows July 2012 silver holding above a support line drawn across the March 2012 low. On April 4, silver closes $2.22 lower and volume increases appropriately. The heavy volume and wide range almost guarantee that the March low will be shattered. Over the next 11 sessions, prices hold within the range of April 4 and make no further downward progress. The largest price bar in this area occurred on April 12. It looked as if a spring were developing. Instead, prices erased all of this gain on the following day. When buyers are absorbing the sellers, upthrusts may occur, but they fail to produce a down-move. In the case of sellers absorbing buyers against a low, the springs fail to materialize. Not all 11 bars are narrow, but certainly the last five days fit the description. The breakdown from these bars begins on April 23 and leads to a $1.88 sell-off in the next

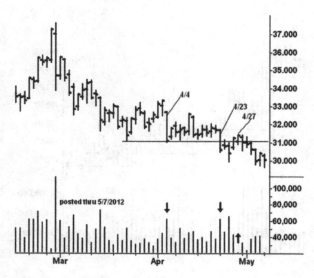

FIGURE 7.7 July 2012 Silver Daily
Source: TradeStation.

few days. On the reflex rally to the April 27 high, the range narrows and volume drops sharply as the market tests the previous breakdown. Prices have fallen below $30 on the last day and hit a low of 26.07 before the July contract expired.

Many Wyckoff students find absorption the most difficult behavior to recognize. The similarity between absorption and a top or bottom formation causes most of the confusion. In *Studies in Tape Reading*, Wyckoff wrote that absorption and distribution represent one of the "opposing forces that are constantly operating in the market."[1] I can find no detailed description by Wyckoff on the subject. It is mentioned in regard to the price action shown in Figure 7.2. Certainly, he knew about the tendency for rising supports and expanding volume on up-swings as well as a market's tendency to hug its lows when the sellers are absorbing the buyers. The other clues I discussed in this chapter are my own observations. Among these, the failure to respond to threatening price action at highs and failed springs at lows are the best indications of absorption.

[1] Rollo Tape [pseud.], *Studies in Tape Reading* (Burlington, VT: Fraser, 1910), 127.

CHAPTER 8

Chart Studies

These chart studies incorporate much of the technical behavior we've already discussed. Some new material is also included. Instead of focusing individually on absorption or springs, let's put it all together. This is how I teach traders my methods. A chart is presented and a question posed: "Would you go long or go short?" When teaching, I have to present situations where something is indeed about to happen. To keep the work honest, some chart situations are not at a point of resolution. This is best, for we don't learn from certainty. Kenko, a fourteenth-century priest and author of *Essays in Idleness*, struck at the heart of the matter when he said, "The most precious thing in life is its uncertainty." Think about it and also the place where certainty reigns.

In Figure 8.1 of Louisiana Pacific, the important support/resistance lines give us a framework for viewing the struggle between the buyers and sellers. The stock made a low at 4.97 on October 30, 2009, and rallied to 6.75 on November 11. After a brief pullback, prices retested 6.75 on day 1, where our study begins. The minor sell-off in the middle of December held well above the October low. Day 12 tells a bullish story: outside upward reversal, price closed near the top of the day's range, it's the strongest close in eight sessions, and volume expanded sharply. The entire advance from day 12 to day 15 displays ease of upward movement and aggressive buying—demand has overcome supply. The buyers are in control. On the move to the high of day 18, however, the volume and daily ranges contract. This says demand has grown tired and the stock is ready for a correction.

A resistance line is drawn across the high of day 18 and a support line three days later. The decline from day 18 to day 21 is a test of the high-volume breakout. Additional tests occurred on days 24, 39, and 45. Springs followed the turnaround after the low of day 24 and 39, but the gains were short lived. Absorption occurred between days 27 and 31, where prices tended to press against the resistance line until they gapped above it on day 32. But the up-move was short lived. The high-volume and outside range on day 33 warned of climactic action. Aggressive selling hit the stock on the next day, and the stock returned to the area between the high of day 1 and the low of day 21. Notice how both lines come within the vertical price range of day 15. From the low of day 39, the stock rallied for three days and suddenly turned down without any warning.

Short-term trades could have been made on several of these price swings but the most apparent trading situation developed after the low of day 45. Here, for the first time, price dipped below the support line and reversed to close above the line and higher than the previous day's close. The volume on day 45 was much lower than the penetrations on day 24 and 39 leading one to believe the selling pressure is dwindling. After the poor performance on day 46, another pullback seems likely. Instead, price holds the next day. If this chart study ended with day 47, we would note the lack of downward follow-through and consider the spring has been tested. A long position would have been warranted with a protective sell stop slightly below 6.75.

As it turned out, the trade took more time to develop. Look at the price action over the next three sessions. On each day (48 through 50), the stock moved below the support line, tested the low of day 45, and recovered to close on a firm note. The clustering of the three closes at the same price underscores the stock's buoyancy and reveals the presence of underlying demand. This is the perfect place to go long. The stock gaps higher on day 51 and then has two inside days. Volume soars on day 53 as the buyer's rev their engines.

This chart study was chosen because it embodies one of my favorite setups: a spring on a pullback to test a breakout. This one begins with a high-volume, accelerated breakout (12 through 15) above a line of resistance. From the initial high of the breakout (18), price corrects into the vertical breakout area where demand overcame supply and a new line (21) of support develops. At some point, a spring (45) of this support line may occur. If prices have tightened—as they did here between 45 and 50—the odds favor a bullish turnaround.

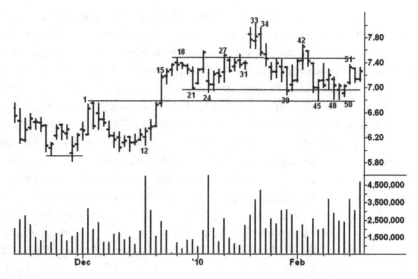

FIGURE 8.1 Louisiana Pacific Daily
Source: TradeStation.

In Figure 8.2 of Arch Coal, we see what appears to be another pullback (15) to test a high-volume vertical area (1). Ultimately, the stock did have a final spring below day 15 that produced a larger rally. But this study deals with reading price bars; special attention is given to the inferences we can draw from the opening price in relation to the high, low, and close. The openings and lows on day 1 through 3 coincided as the stock rallied vigorously. On day 4, however, the stock opened above the previous day and reversed to close near its low: the first bearish change in behavior. Volatility increased on day 6 as the stock opened below the previous day's low, rebounded above the high of day 4 and closed below the midpoint of the range with a mere 12-cent gain. After an obligatory bounce on day 7, the stock falls to a temporary low on day 9. The following four sessions hold within the range of day 9 as trading activity subsides. Day 13 opens above the highs of the previous three days, breaks below the low of the previous day, and closes lower. This outside day says to expect further weakness.

At the close of day 15, nothing bullish can be made out of the price movement. The stock opened down, rallied above unchanged only to succumb on the close. On the next day, price gaps higher and moves steadily upward to close on a strong note. One of the strongest springs occurs with an upward gap following a demoralizing breakdown below support. Within the up-move, price repeatedly gaps lower (day 20 thru 25) but recovers to close near the daily highs. This persistent buoyancy tells us demand remains strong. The trend changes on day 27. Here price opens higher, breaks the previous low and closes down: the first outside, downward reversal since day 13. The bearish picture becomes clearer after day 28 where we see the same volatile price movement as on day 6. Similar behavior occurs on day 30, but, to make matters worse, the stock closes below the previous day's low. On the next day, the stock suffers its largest sell-off as prices plunge below the axis line drawn across the high of day 4. This breakdown trapped the longs who bought above the axis line. When the stock later recovered to test this line (days 35, 43, and 48), the openings were strong but the closings weak.

Day 35 stands out with its huge range and volume. It could have been either a sign of weakness or climactic action. As it turned out, there was little downward follow-through and the stock stabilized. True to form, the higher opening on day 36 led to a little more weakness, but this time it recovered on the close (unlike day 30, 31, 32, 33, and 35). On the up-move to day 48, the rallies on day 38, 40, and 43 fail to hold; one might infer the large operators are using strength to unload stock. The same can be said about day 48 but here it is more damaging because the rally fails along the axis line. (If I wanted to make a point-and-figure projection off this chart, it would be made from the high at 48.) The reversal action on day 51 sealed the bearish story.

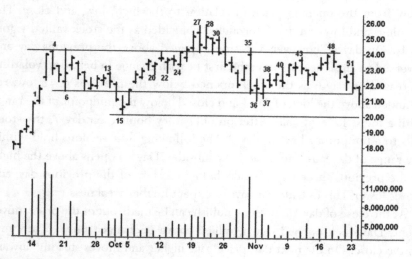

FIGURE 8.2 Arch Coal Daily
Source: TradeStation.

Several sections of Wyckoff's course dealt with U.S. Steel. He would view Figure 8.3 as a tour de force of market behavior. In a capsule, we see the buying climax on day 47, where the volume was the heaviest in six months and the range stretched to its largest size since December 2008. High volume on the next two days signaled the presence of supply. A low-volume, secondary test occurred on day 53. The next day's drop below the low of day 53 shows that the buyers have removed their bids. Wyckoff would point to day 55 as the "decisive breaking of the very backbone of the advance." Steady supply pounds prices lower on days 56, 58, 59, 60, and 61. Collectively, the last three days represent a selling climax, with shortening of the thrust at the end. The decline from the high has returned to the point where the stock shifted into a steeper trend in early December. The sellers are unable to keep prices down on day 66 after the stock falls below support. Increased volume tells us demand has resurfaced. Over the next three sessions, the stock trades in a minor three-point range, and the rising supports point toward a bullish resolution. It comes on day 70, where the stock rises above the last five days' highs.

Wyckoff's main trading tools were the ticker tape (from which he made wave charts), point-and-figure charts, and, later in life, bar charts with volume. His indicator for depicting stock market activity was based on the number of inches per hour the ticker tape traveled—an ingenious idea that would be impractical today where an hour's ticker tape might span the length of a football field. I believe Wyckoff would see the value of the tick difference indicator plotted as a histogram on Figure 8.3. (Actual volume is used, not tick volume.) It shows the difference between the up and down volume per time period. Not all of the readings are meaningful, so I place greater emphasis on the larger readings. From day 1 to day 47, net buying dominated the advance. The narrow range on day 46 attracted little volume but the net up-volume was the largest reading to date. I would assume this large influx of buying is short covering and weak longs sensing the stock is still headed higher. On days 48 and 49, the big jump in net down-volume indicates the stock is meeting supply; it reinforces the bearish message of the heavy total volumes. The higher close and surge in net up-volume on day 53 suggest that the stock is ready to move higher. But the lack of follow-through on day 54 puts the stock in jeopardy. On day 55, the die is cast: ease of downward movement and heavy volume. Day 58 has heavy volume, ease of downward movement, and a large increase in net down-volume as longs flee. The selling reaches a crescendo on day 59, where the volume exceeds 45 million shares. Notice here, too, the large net up-volume (1.2 million shares); it says the short covering and new buying are greater than the long liquidation.

Only one horizontal line is drawn across the chart, and it is on one of these so-called crisscross areas. The high on day 13 was tested (i.e., criss-crossed) on days 24, 25, and 26. Support later formed along this line between days 61 and 66. On day 66, the low of day 61 is penetrated and the stock reverses upward. Three days of lateral movement are resolved on day 70, where the stock closes above recent highs on large net up-volume. Equally heavy up-volume pushes prices higher on the next day. U.S. Steel then returns to its January 2010 high.

I mentioned the true range in the previous study without much explanation. In an uptrend, it encompasses the distance from the previous close to the current day's high. Thus, the true range includes gaps. The true range in a downtrend spans the distance from the previous day's close to the next bar's low. I have observed how a large true range often coincides with heavy volume. I have previously shown how true range can serve as a proxy for volume and especially for markets or yield indices where no volume data are available.

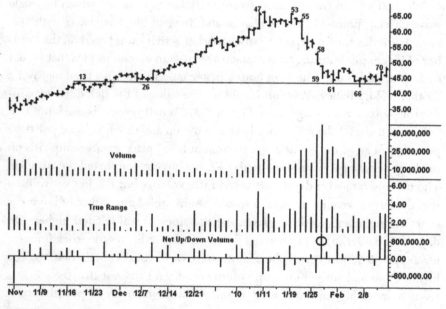

FIGURE 8.3 U.S. Steel Daily
Source: TradeStation.

Figure 8.4 of the daily sterling/yen cross-rate illustrates the point nicely. Through the true-range histogram, a thin line is drawn along the 300-pip level. A range of this size or greater is used to define ease of movement.

Thirteen days have a range of 300 pips or more. Only three of these days (7, 11, and 70) closed higher. Day 25 and 58 did not have wide ranges, but they play an important role in reading the chart.

Starting from day 1, we see ease of downward movement followed by stopping action on day 2. The position of the close on day 2 indicates buying emerged. The lengthening of the range on day 7 was climactic and heavy selling drove the rate lower on day 9. The selling pressure stopped on the next day and the cross-rate rose to a slight new high on day 25 where the range narrowed. The weakness and lack of follow through on day 26 warned of an upthrust and fresh supply struck on day 27. Over the next 12 days, the buyers attempted to absorb through the overhead supply without success. Then came the sharp downturn on days 39 and 42.

The attempt to spring on day 46 faltered after the weak response on the next two days. These two narrow ranges with poor closes offer an ideal shorting opportunity. The large breakdown on day 49 must have been accompanied by heavy volume. It and day 50 find support along the line drawn across the low of day 2. Although the action on days 49 and 50 temporarily stops the decline, they portend greater weakness. The daily ranges (shall we say volume) stay below 250 pips on the rebound to day 58. Now the rally has tested the breakdown point and shows no willingness to continue higher. Ease of downward movement begins on day 62 and accelerates on days 64 and 66. Volume had to be climactic at the low of this decline. Also, the currency pair reached an oversold position within its downtrend. Day 70 turns the trend.

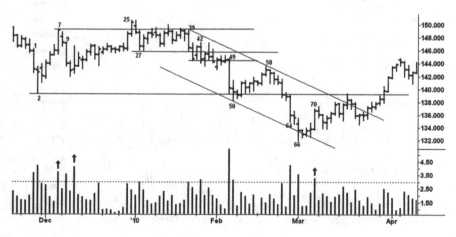

FIGURE 8.4   Sterling/Yen Daily
Source: TradeStation.

Here, we have the widest range on an up-bar since day 7. The two buy points were the selling climax on day 66 and the pullback on days 72 and 73.

I mentioned earlier how forex traders have no actual volume data. But they do have access to tick volume on intraday charts. Tick volume measures the number of transactions in a given time period. It does not reveal the number of contracts traded on each transaction; therefore, it really reflects trading activity. On the five-minute chart of the sterling/yen cross-rate (Figure 8.5), I have plotted the tick volume as a line above the true-range histogram. You can readily see how the peaks and valleys of the true range dovetail nicely with the tick volume. Below the true range, I have placed the net up/down volume differences. A cumulative line of these differences is plotted atop the bar chart. It shows the trend of the net volume. The cumulative line differs from on-balance volume, which is based on up or down closes.

Figure 8.5 shows the sterling/yen cross-rate on March 8, 2010. Here, we see a trading range during the morning resolved by an upthrust in the period prior to bar 1. Bar 2 is a bearish change in behavior as the range widens to 30 pips, the net down-volume swells to −99 ticks, and the total tick volume equals 441. All three readings were new highs to date. Between bars 3 and 6 there is no ability to rally, and net down-volumes remain heavy on

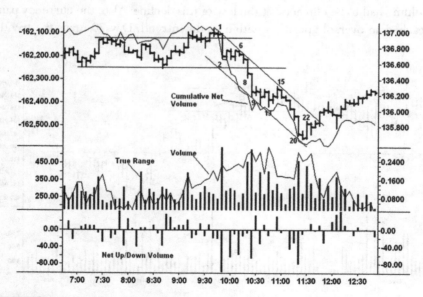

FIGURE 8.5   Sterling/Yen Five-Minute Chart
Source: TradeStation.

the two small down-bars. The bottom falls out on bars 8 and 9, where the wide ranges and heavy volume indicate that supply has overcome demand. Temporary support forms on bar 11. This bar's low was penetrated on bar 13, where we see the day's largest tick volume (546). The big effort to take the market lower and the midrange close on bar 13 suggested a spring might occur. It failed on bar 15 against the supply line of the down-channel, and the cross-rate closed lower in each of the next six periods. The large range and net down volume smacked of climactic action (bar 20) near the bottom of the down-channel. Demand surfaced on bar 22, where we have the largest true range on an up-bar since the decline began. This change in behavior provided a low-risk buying opportunity. There are only seven up-bars within the sell-off from bar 1 to bar 22. Because the net up-volumes on these seven bars were so low compared to the net down-volumes, the cumulative net volume trended in lock step with price. As a point of interest, March 8, 2010, corresponds to bar 71 in Figure 8.4.

CHAPTER 9

Tape Reading Part I

In his autobiography, Wyckoff tells the story of how he began studying the tape. He had observed some of the largest traders of the day sitting alone in their offices silently reading the ticker tape. He realized that the secret door to success lies in learning this technique. He concluded this discussion by saying, "In consideration of those who believe that tape reading is an obsolete practice, I affirm that knowledge of it is the most valuable equipment a Wall Street trader can possess."[1] He added, "If I were beginning my Wall Street career now, and knew what forty years of it have taught me, I should apply myself first of all to this business of judging and forecasting the stock market by its own action."[2] For purposes of tape reading, Wyckoff devised a wave chart and special point-and-figure charts that included volume. It's no coincidence that the first chapter in the Wyckoff course that discusses charts is entitled "Buying and Selling Waves." In the beginning of this chapter, he tells the student to hereafter "think in waves."

I have never watched the flow of orders on a ticker tape. In my first two years in the futures business, all of the charts were handmade. Intraday charting involved maintaining a point-and-figure chart or constructing an hourly chart from the price changes on a wall-size quote board with

---

[1] Richard D. Wyckoff, *Wall Street Ventures and Adventures* (New York: Greenwood Press, 1968), 178.

[2] Ibid., 179.

moveable parts. We phoned the exchange floor and someone read the hourly volumes off a chalkboard where all price data were posted. The nature of my work has kept me in front of the market for 42 years.

Buyers and sellers are locked in a perpetual struggle for dominance. Buying waves are followed by selling waves in a seesaw battle until one side gains the upper hand. It can be compared to an arm-wrestling contest in which one person attempts to overcome the force—the "pulling power"—of the other. If we could attach electrodes to the combatants' arms and view physiological readings on blood pressure, sodium levels, cholesterol, and the like, we could look for the subtle signs of strength that telegraph when one side is gaining the upper hand. It is the same in tape reading. We judge the amount of effort (i.e., volume), the reward for that effort, the ease of movement, and so on to determine when short-term and intermediate changes in trend are about to occur. Intraday charts are best suited for finding short-term trend reversals. The trick is to use intraday charts with the most accurate picture of price/volume behavior.

In the early days of Wall Street, all intraday information was transmitted on the ticker tape. Point-and-figure charts were popular among technical traders. If one plotted every $\frac{1}{8}$-point fluctuation in a stock, an entire day's price action could be reproduced. Solely from a point-and-figure chart, one can recognize levels of support and resistance, draw trend lines and channels, and make price projections. While this is useful information, it is volume that tells a logical story of what is taking place in a market and alerts one when it is at a turning point. Humphrey Neill aptly wrote in 1931: "Tape interpretation depends upon consideration of the action of the volume . . . . The action of the volume tells us of the supply and demand; price merely denotes the value of the volume."[3] For a more accurate picture of intraday price action in a single stock, Richard Wyckoff devised a volume figure chart. A crude sketch of the volume figure chart first appeared in *Studies in Tape Reading*.[4] Years later, Wyckoff wrote a course on tape reading where the volume figure chart (renamed the tape reading chart) was discussed in detail. Since the construction of my own wave chart, called the Weis Wave, is an outgrowth of Wyckoff's tape reading chart, it makes for an appropriate starting point.

Figure 9.1 is a remake of Wyckoff's volume-figure chart showing all the movement in AT&T on June 2, 1932. It was included in his original tape reading course, which is still available (but modified) from the Stock Market Institute

---

[3] Humphrey B. Neill, *Tape Reading and Market Tactics* (Burlington, VT: Fraser Publishing, 1970), 118.

[4] Rollo Tape [pseud.], *Studies in Tape Reading* (Burlington, VT: Fraser, 1910), 124.

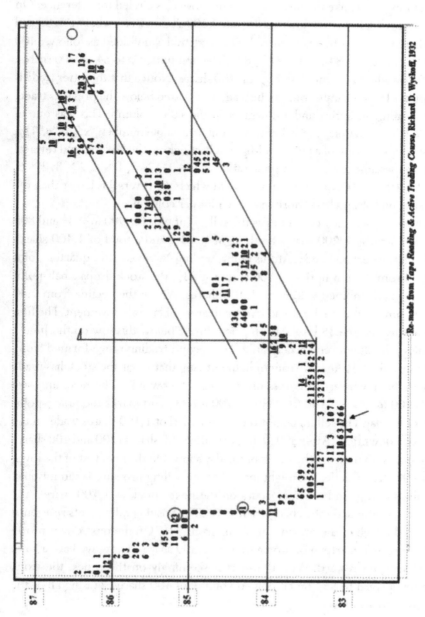

FIGURE 9.1 AT&T Tape Reading Chart, June 2, 1932

in Phoenix, Arizona. We immediately notice the absence of the x's and o's that normally comprise a point-and-figure chart. In their place are numbers representing the hundreds of shares traded on every $\frac{1}{8}$ -point fluctuation. Whenever consecutive trades occurred at the same price, Wyckoff totaled the volume. We see that AT&T closed on June 1 at $85\frac{1}{8}$, where volume totaled 2,300 shares. The closing price, like the next day's opening price, is circled for reference. On June 2, the stock gapped down to $84\frac{1}{4}$ on 3,100 shares. Zeroes between 85 and $84\frac{3}{8}$ show where no trades occurred. The next trades unfolded as follows: 400 @ $84\frac{1}{8}$ . . . 600 @ 84 . . . 1,100 @ $83\frac{7}{8}$. The first uptick is to 84 on 300 shares. It is followed by a downtick to $83\frac{7}{8}$ on 100 shares. Notice that the latter trade is not plotted in a separate column. Instead, it is plotted below the previous trade, thus creating an uptick and a downtick in the same column. This was one of Wyckoff's innovations. No column can contain a single number, "x," or "o." This is the unique feature of a point-and-figure chart, where the box size and reversal unit are the same (i.e., a one-to-one ratio). A 1×2, 1×3, 1×6, 2×8, 2×6, 5×15, 100×300, or any combination in which the reversal is larger than the box size, will always have more than one plot per column.

The wave of selling continues as the sellers hit bids for 900 @ $83\frac{3}{4}$ and 800 @ $83\frac{5}{8}$. A meager 200 shares are bought at $83\frac{3}{4}$, and a total of 1,400 shares trade on the decline to $83\frac{1}{4}$. At this point, trading narrows into a quarter-point range. From the last uptick of 100 shares at $83\frac{3}{8}$, the stock drops a half-point to $82\frac{7}{8}$ on a combined volume of 1,400 shares. Within the decline from 2:30 P.M. on June 1, the stock has had two small areas of lateral movement. The first formed around the 85 level. When prices broke below this low on the June 2 opening, the downtrend accelerated. The second trading range formed along and above the $83\frac{1}{4}$ line. We cannot help noticing that so far the stock has made only slight downward progress on the break below $83\frac{1}{4}$. The next up-wave reads 100 @ 83 . . . 100 @ $83\frac{1}{8}$ . . . 700 @ $83\frac{1}{4}$ and marks the first $\frac{3}{8}$-point rally of the day. The sellers do not retreat as a total of 1,100 shares trade on the next two downticks. After 300 @ $83\frac{1}{8}$, another 700 shares (300 and 400 shares consecutively) trade on the retest of the day's low. On the final test of the lows, only 400 shares trade. We might infer that the selling pressure is diminishing. A bullish change in behavior occurs on the next uptick as 1,700 shares (the largest up-volume on the chart) trade at 83. The ensuing rally meets resistance at $83\frac{1}{4}$, the high of the previous upswing from $82\frac{7}{8}$. On the next down-move, AT&T drops a quarter-point on a total of 1,300 shares. Here, we have a large effort with no reward. With the market seemingly on the ropes, the stock flutters upward to $83\frac{3}{8}$ on combined volume of 400 shares, erasing all of the previous down-move.

Evidence mounts for a trend reversal: the slight progress below the second congestion area indicates that the downward momentum is lessening; the lower volume on the last test of the low suggests the selling pressure is tiring; the large increase in volume (1,700 shares) that emerged on an uptick reveals the presence of demand; the final break to 83 failed to attract new selling, and the effortless rally off the low said the selling is spent. After the last test of $82\frac{7}{8}$ and subsequent rally to $83\frac{1}{4}$, Wyckoff, in his reading of this chart, said to lower stops on any short position to $83\frac{3}{4}$ and place a buy stop at the same price in order to go long. His protective sell stop was placed at $82\frac{5}{8}$, one quarter-point below the day's low. He noted the combined 6,300 shares that traded along the 83 and $82\frac{7}{8}$ lines and the stock's unwillingness to give ground after the two tests of the low. Once the stock rallied to $83\frac{1}{4}$, the bundle of 6,300 shares was viewed as potential accumulation in the context of one day's trading.

After the stock rallied to $83\frac{3}{8}$, the next 18 price changes are confined to a narrow range. The unwillingness of the stock to move lower indicates it is on the springboard for a larger up-wave. It begins with 1,200 @ $83\frac{1}{2}$ and continues without interruption until reaching 84. A total of 4,500 shares are taken on this breakout. The ease of upward movement accompanied by an increase in volume is a sign of strength that begins the markup from a base area. Because Wyckoff's tape reading chart is constructed like a point-and-figure chart, it can be used for making price projections. As with any point-and-figure chart, one counts the number of boxes or trades plotted along a line of congestion and multiplies the total by the reversal unit. The AT&T chart is $\frac{1}{8} \times \frac{1}{8}$; therefore, the number of boxes is multiplied by $\frac{1}{8}$. (With a 1×3 point-and-figure chart, the length of the congestion area is multiplied by 3.) Counting from right to left and from the last downtick (400 shares) on the $83\frac{3}{8}$ line, we have 24 boxes: $24 \times \frac{1}{8} = 3$; $3 + 83\frac{3}{8} = 86\frac{3}{8}$. Point-and-figure counts are purely mechanical and have no magical powers. Sometimes they have pinpoint accuracy, and other times they fail miserably. No trade should be established solely because of point-and-figure counts. They represent potential. Congestion areas on point-and-figure charts theoretically depict the amount of cause or preparation that has been built for a potential move. When point-and-figure counts are fulfilled, a day trader or swing trader may want to adjust protective stops, take partial profits, or simply become more vigilant for signs of ending action.

After the breakout to 84, there is active pumping action as 1,200 shares trade on the decline to $83\frac{3}{4}$, 700 on the rebound to 84, and 800 on the dip to $83\frac{7}{8}$. It is caused by some longs taking quick profits, liquidation by buyers who bought the opening and are thankful to recoup most of their earlier loss, and new shorts selling against the opening high in hope of another downswing. That the stock gives little ground in the face of this selling says the buyers are absorbing the supply around the 84 level. The next upswing carries the stock to $84\frac{3}{8}$ on combined volume of 1,600 shares. Another shallow correction ensues before it ends with 100 shares at $84\frac{1}{8}$—the first downtick on 100 shares since the stock moved off the $83\frac{3}{8}$ congestion line. It reflects a lack of selling pressure. The sellers raise their offerings from $84\frac{1}{8}$ to $84\frac{1}{2}$, where 600 shares are bought. One hundred shares are bought at $84\frac{5}{8}$ prior to a downtick to $84\frac{1}{2}$ on 1,100 shares. The latter transaction catches the tape reader's attention, as it draws out the most amount of selling since shortly after the opening. It warns that the stock is beginning to encounter supply. The supply may be profit taking by longs; we don't know. The stock rallies to $84\frac{3}{4}$ on a meager 300 shares. A shortening of the upward progress and dwindling of upside volume say demand is tiring. The tape reader raises stops to $83\frac{3}{8}$. There is no supply on the quick break to $84\frac{1}{2}$, but demand remains weak on the next rally (100 shares @ $84\frac{5}{8}$). Then renewed supply emerges as the stock drops to $84\frac{1}{8}$ on combined volume of 2,000 shares. A $\frac{1}{8}$-point uptick is followed by another 1,700 shares on the decline to 84, but there is little reward for the effort and we infer that buying is present. The next rally from 84 to $84\frac{1}{2}$ on 1,900 shares says demand is growing. On the ensuing downswing to 84, the combined volume is 2,200 shares. The lack of downward follow-through attests to the presence of demand once more. We have seen on earlier chart studies how prices often pull back to test previous high-volume areas where demand overcame supply (i.e., the rally from 83 $\frac{3}{8}$ to 84) or where the buyers absorbed through overhead supply. After the effervescent rally from 84 to $84\frac{3}{8}$, only 100 shares trade on the decline to $84\frac{1}{4}$. The force of the selling is exhausted—once again the stock is poised to rally. ("Anyone who can spot these points has much to win and little to lose.") Additional shares could be purchased on the uptick to $84\frac{3}{8}$ and all stops raised to $83\frac{3}{4}$. In fairness to Wyckoff, he made no reference to adding shares, nor did he discuss the point-and-figure counts.

The stock has a vertical run to $85\frac{1}{4}$ on combined volume of 3,300 shares as the buyers overwhelm the sellers. We now can draw an uptrend line from the last low at $83\frac{3}{8}$ to the latest low at 84. A parallel line is drawn across the intervening high at $84\frac{3}{4}$. But the steep angle of advance has driven prices beyond the supply line of the up-channel, creating an overbought condition. The stock ignores the channel and continues higher after a minor sell-off to 85. This upswing reaches $85\frac{1}{2}$ on combined volume of 1,600 shares. Demand slackens slightly, but there is no sign of supply. There is no pressure on the downtick to $85\frac{3}{8}$. But demand is obviously tired on the next upswing: 100 @ $85\frac{5}{8}$ . . . 100 @ $85\frac{3}{4}$. The stock drops $\frac{1}{4}$ point on combined volume of 800 shares as the sellers flex their muscle. Fresh buy orders for 1,500 shares produce a retest of the high, but there is no reward for the effort. The minor support around the $85\frac{3}{8}$ line quickly gives way as the stock slips to 85 $\frac{1}{8}$ on 1,000 shares. A two-way struggle develops as the buyers attempt to absorb the selling. It ends with a last-gasp purchase of 300 shares at $85\frac{5}{8}$ before prices topple $1\frac{1}{8}$ points to $84\frac{1}{2}$. About this sell-off, Wyckoff wrote one line: "Pressure on the decline is neither light nor heavy; it is a normal reaction." He considers the decline "normal" because it does not retrace 50 percent or more of the advance from $82\frac{7}{8}$. But it comes close. A point-and-figure count can be made across the seven plots along the $85\frac{5}{8}$ line for a decline to $84\frac{3}{4}$; however, it is slightly exceeded. The decline stops along the demand line of the up-channel. In addition, support forms on top of the previous resistance area between $84\frac{3}{4}$ and $84\frac{5}{8}$ and within the vertical price rise. In a statement reminiscent of profile analysis, Wyckoff described the tape reading chart as "particularly valuable in showing the quantity of stock at various levels." The total number of shares traded above $85\frac{3}{8}$ is 8,300. If the 6,300 shares traded between 83 and $82\frac{7}{8}$ could be viewed as minor accumulation, the heavy volume above 8,300 can be considered to be distribution. In light of this stopping action plus the overbought position of the stock within the up-channel, profits on the second purchase at $84\frac{3}{8}$ should be taken after the last-gasp rally to $85\frac{5}{8}$.

From the low at $84\frac{1}{2}$, there is very little time to react. A rebound to $84\frac{7}{8}$ and downtick to $84\frac{3}{4}$ lead to a vertical run to $86\frac{1}{2}$. As soon as this liftoff accelerated, we would raise the stop on the original purchase to $84\frac{3}{4}$. We would also broaden the up-channel by drawing a parallel line across the $85\frac{3}{4}$ high. Yet, at $86\frac{1}{2}$, an overbought condition already exists. The steep angle of advance, the combined volume of 5,200 shares on this vertical up-move, and the overbought condition spell climactic action. (Notice that 2,300 of the 5,200 volume occurred above 86, suggesting that the stock was beginning to encounter selling.) If the long position is not immediately closed out, stops should be raised to $85\frac{5}{8}$, just below the previous high at $85\frac{3}{4}$. Next, the stock drops to 86 on sales of 600, 700 and 200 shares. Look carefully at the character of the final up-wave to $86\frac{7}{8}$. The combined volume of 4,400 shares is rewarded with only a $\frac{3}{8}$-point gain. When the upward thrust shortens and volume increases, we know price has met selling. Unless one was trading a larger situation not visible on the chart provided here, trades established at $83\frac{3}{8}$ should be closed out. Wyckoff noted in his commentary that 10,000 shares traded at $86\frac{1}{2}$ and above before the correction to $86\frac{1}{8}$. Volume increases as traders even up their positions on the close, but there is little downward progress. The shallowness of the correction testified that the buyers absorbed the fresh supply, and the stock rallied to $89\frac{1}{2}$ on June 3.

Wyckoff's volume-figure chart was used to read the intraday flow of orders into an individual stock. To follow the broader market, Wyckoff plotted an intraday wave chart of five leading stocks taken from separate groups. He calculated the aggregate price of these stocks as they ebbed and flowed throughout a trading session. The resulting wave chart broke each day into separate buying and selling waves. Wyckoff compared the length, duration, volume, and activity on these waves to determine the dominant trend and to locate the early clues that pointed to a change in trend. The same behavior we observed on the volume-figure chart can be found on the wave chart. One can see shortening of the upward or downward thrust, ease of movement, stopping volume, the interaction with trend lines and support/resistance lines, and so on. While Wyckoff's wave chart of market leaders (today it is known as the Wyckoff Wave) is still maintained by the Stock Market Institute, it has undergone many changes over the years. With the advent of stock index futures, however, the need for a wave chart of market leaders seems less compelling. But a wave chart can be useful in the study of individual stocks or futures. In his tape reading course, Wyckoff recommended keeping wave charts of individual stocks, although I cannot find an example in any of his published writings. As will be shown, a wave chart of a single stock or futures contract can be constructed from every price change. As I experimented with volume-figure charts (or tape reading charts), a method for converting the information into waves evolved.

There is no difference between a wave chart and a volume-figure chart whenever the price scale equals the minimum fluctuation of a market. When I first experimented with the idea of making a wave chart, I converted Wyckoff's volume figure chart of AT&T into a continuous line. This removed the ambiguity of having an uptick and a downtick in the same column. More important, it allowed me to total the volume on the swings larger than $\frac{1}{8}$ point and thus provide a better picture of where the stock encountered supply and demand. One drawback, however, is this modification increases the size of the chart. For a modern-day market, with thousands of intraday price changes, such a chart would be impractical. My final rendition is presented in Figure 9.2, where the high-volume areas are vividly apparent. I immediately decided that some of the data should be filtered. The easiest way to filter data is to increase the size of a minimum wave. I modified the volume-figure chart into a wave chart with a $\frac{1}{8}$-point scale and a $\frac{1}{4}$-point wave or reversal. This filters out all of the $\frac{1}{8}$-point reactions within a wave, removes having an uptick and downtick in the same column and reduces the size of the chart. It works just like a $\frac{1}{8} \times \frac{1}{4}$ point-and-figure chart in which the box size is $\frac{1}{8}$ and the reversal is $\frac{1}{4}$. This makes the information clearer.

With the aid of this chart, the story jumps out at us. First, we see the 2,800 shares on the test of the day's low where the large effort yields no downward follow-through. The next two rallies on 2700 and 2,800 shares speak of aggressive buying. The 5,800 shares on the breakout to 84 starts the mark-up. Later, after the 4200 share sell-off to 84, the selling pressure is

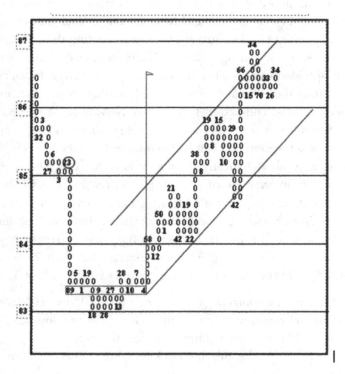

FIGURE 9.2 AT&T Modified Tape Reading Chart, June 2, 1932

half as large on the 2200 retest. On the next up-wave to $85\frac{3}{4}$, the up-volume (1900) drops to the lowest level since the markup began. This warns of an impending downturn. Three waves later, on the rise to $85\frac{5}{8}$, the larger 2,900 volume shows a large buying effort with no reward. It, too, indicates that a sell-off is imminent. Although this chart was made from 1932 price/volume data, the behavior has not changed over the past 80 years. It's truly fascinating to see the same action recurring over and over on these charts. Although I was once ridiculed for saying this, I compare the beauty of this repetitive behavior to sunrises and sunsets. In Chapter 11, all of the behavior we have discussed here will appear on stock, futures, and forex charts. While some of the subtler information on Wyckoff's $\frac{1}{8} \times \frac{1}{8}$ volume-figure chart may be missing here, one adept at reading price/volume behavior would have no difficulty interpreting and trading from Figure 9.2.

As we have seen, Wyckoff's volume figure chart was constructed from every transaction. In the 1990s, trade-by-trade volume data were not available on bond futures. As a result, we used tick volume, and the numbers were very small. In order to assign a volume per trade, I decided to consider every "trade" during the day as the close at the end of each one-minute time period. This limited the data surveyed for constructing the chart (day session only) to 400 price changes (i.e., 400 minutes per day), and, more important, it provided a volume reading for each price change. I then created a data sheet listing the 400 minutes within each trading session. Whenever the same price occurred consecutively, I totaled the volume. If one constructs a volume-figure chart from one-minute closing prices and no consecutive closings occur at the same price, it is conceivable 400 data points will appear in one session. While statistically possible, it never occurred.

Figure 9.3 is an example of a $\frac{1}{32} \times \frac{1}{32}$ tape reading chart constructed from one-minute closings. Since it has a 1:1 ratio between the scale and the reversal, an up-tick and down-tick can occur in the same column as on Figure 9.1. The following list (tape) itemizes the price changes on November 29, 1993, in the December 1993 bond contract between 7:20 A.M. and 8:48 A.M. CST. On the previous day, the contract closed at 11603.

> *7:20 11612-6:* The contract gaps higher from 11603 to 11612. Since the opening price continues an up-move from the previous day, we plot zeroes within the same column to reflect the gap.
> *7:21 11611-11:* We plot this downtick in the next chart column.
> *7:22 11613-10*

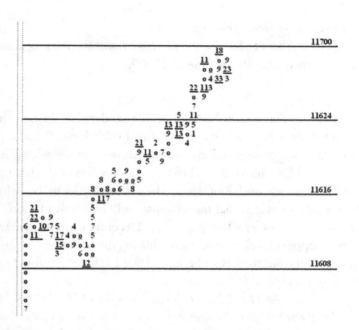

FIGURE 9.3 December 1993 Bonds One-Tick Tape Reading Chart

7:23 11613-12: We enter the plots only after a price change occurs, for there may be consecutive one-minute closes at the same price. When this occurs, plot the total volume. Enter the volume (22) above the previous plot at 11611. Remember, there must be at least two numbers in a column. Since we have only one downtick to 11611 in this column, enter the uptick to 11613 above it.

7:24 11614-11

7:25 11614-10

7:26 11612-10: After this price change, we enter the 21 ticks at 11614 above the 22 ticks at 11613. In 1993, anyone familiar with intraday bond volume would view the sharp increase over the previous four minutes as evidence the opening rally has run its course. The large buying effort netted only $\frac{1}{32}$nd above the opening high.

7:27 11613-9; 7:28 11612-7; 7:29:11611-7; 7:30 11612-5: Since the high at 11614, the volume on the two upticks (see underlined times) diminished to 9 and 5, respectively. A tape reader would notice the weaker demand on these upticks, which indicates that the sell-off has not ended.

7:31 11611-11; 7:32 11611-6 [total 17]; 7:33 11610-9; 7:34: 11610-6 [total 15]; 7:35 11609-3: A flurry of selling on combined down-volume of 35.

7:36 11611-4; a zero is placed at 11610

7:37 1610-3; 7:38 11610-4; 7:39 11610-2 [total 9]: Trading activity has slowed down after the decline to 11609.

7:40 11612-4

7:41 11609-6

7:42 11610-1: The 11609 line has been tested twice. In real time, we would draw a support line across the 11609 level. Volume remains light, thus suggesting that the selling pressure is dwindling. A minor downtrend line drawn from 11614 across the top of the last uptick to 11612 creates a wedge or apex. The narrowing of price swings into such a pattern warns that the stalemate will be resolved soon.

7:43 11608-6; 7:44 11608-6 [total 12]: December bonds penetrate the 11609 support level, momentarily shifting the advantage to the sellers. The sell-off from the 11614 high to 11608 has taken 24 minutes. Watch the action in the next five minutes.

7:45 11611-5; 7:46 11612-7; 7:47 11613-5; 7:48 11614-5; 7:49 11616-8: No downward follow-through as prices take big steps upward to a new high. The easy upward movement signals a bullish change in behavior, and the tape reader buys bonds. Protective sell stops are placed at 11607.

Following the rise to 11616, bonds hold above the previous high at 11614 without giving anyone an opportunity to buy cheaply. The rally continues in stair-step fashion. A burst of volume (21 ticks) temporarily stops the advance at 11621. The first effort to push above 11624 is thwarted because longs typically take profits around the quarter-point increments. Once the profit taking is absorbed, prices rise from 11621 to 11630 (8:21 to 8:31) with only one downtick. The market's proximity to 11700 entices more profit taking. Bonds have almost rallied to the top of the up-channel drawn from the low of the previous correction. In addition, most of the point-and-figure projection across the 11527 line has been fulfilled. Yet we see no evidence of supply overcoming demand. Now let's read the tape from the 8:31 high at 11630:

8:32 11628-4; 8:33 11627-3: This low-volume correction reflects no aggressive selling.

8:34 11628-7; 8:35 11628-8; 8:36 11628-4; 8:37 11628-8; 8:38 11628-6: The market trades for five minutes and gains only $\frac{1}{32}$nd despite the day's largest block of volume (33). This clustering of one-minute closing prices at 11628 says the market is having difficulty making upward progress.

8:39 11629-9; 8:40 11631-8; 8:41 11631-10 [18 total]: From the low at 11627, bonds rally to 11631, one tick above the 8:31 high, on combined volume of 60: a small reward for the large effort. This up-wave spans $\frac{4}{32}$nds but only gains $\frac{1}{32}$nd above the previous high. The volume is greater than on the rally from 11608 to 11616 and on the up-wave from 11621 to 11627. The lack of upward progress in the face of such a large effort tells us the bond market has encountered supply. We either raise the sell-stop to 11628 on the long position or close out the trade immediately. Now comes the first evidence that the sellers are overcoming the buyers.

8:42 11630-9

8:43 11629-3; 8:44 11629-4; 8:45 11629-8; 8:46 11629-4; 8:47 11629-4 [total 23]; 8:48 11628-3: The total volume at 11629 is the largest on a downtick since November 28. The sell-off from 11631 to 11628 is accompanied by the largest volume since the 11608 low.

A bond $\frac{1}{32}$nd volume-figure chart requires a data sheet of one-minute closes and volumes plus chart paper with a grid large enough to enter the volume numbers. Anyone who has the patience to make such a chart and intensely study intraday price movement will learn a great deal about how markets work. Although greatly modified, the concept behind this chart stems from Wyckoff's tape reading course. Its interpretation, however, is mostly a matter of simple logic gained through study and observation. From a logical reading of the tape, one gains a sense, a feel for what will happen next.

In Figure 9.3, look at the rise from the last low at 11621 where the volume equaled 4 ticks. From this low, bonds gained $\frac{9}{32}$nds with only one downtick. The thrust shortened on the final up-wave, and it had volume of 60 ticks, the heaviest reading for the day. The 35-tick volume on the next down-wave was the heaviest since the spring low. It doesn't take a rocket scientist to understand the message. In *Studies in Tape Reading*, Wyckoff wrote:

> Tape Reading is rapid-fire horse sense. . . . The Tape Reader aims to make deductions from each succeeding transaction—every shift of the market's kaleidoscope; to grasp a new situation, force it lightning-like through the weighing machine of the brain, and to reach a decision which will be acted upon with coolness and precision.[5]

To requote from his autobiography, *Wall Street Ventures and Adventures*, Wyckoff said:

> The purpose of the self-training and continued application of the methods suggested in *Studies in Tape Reading* was to develop an

---

[5] Tape [pseud.], *Studies in Tape Reading*, 10.

intuitive judgment [my emphasis], which would be the natural outcome of spending twenty-seven hours a week at the ticker over many months and years.[6]

The "methods" he refers to are examples of how he logically read the ticker tape. By no means am I trying to slight the information he imparts. Wyckoff knew tape reading cannot be reduced to a set of specific instructions. It's like dancing. You can learn the basic dance steps, but in order to dance you must have the feel of the music. Wyckoff's tape reading course explained the construction of the tape reading chart, and he showed how it could be integrated with a wave chart of market leaders. When Wyckoff began studying markets, there were no intraday quotes on the Dow or other indices. A single, closing figure at the end of each trading session was the only measure of a day's performance. As already noted, Wyckoff created a wave chart of five or six leading stocks. He plotted the volume on the buying and selling waves, thus making it very useful for judging the condition of the overall market. It is interesting to note that Wyckoff chose to present the data as a wave chart rather than a 5- or 60-minute bar chart. A tape reader would know price movement unfolds in waves rather than in equal time periods.

An entire $\frac{1}{32}$nd volume-figure chart of bonds is too unwieldy for showing a continuum of price history. But if we change the reversal unit to $\frac{3}{32}$ nds, we can reduce the number of wave turns per day. For example, the complete $\frac{1}{32}$nd chart on November 29, 1993, had 258 out of a maximum 400 waves. In Figure 9.4, the modified reversal size reduces the number of reversals (let's call them waves) to 32. This $\frac{3}{32}$nd wave chart constructed from the same one-minute closes as on Figure 9.3 tells a wonderful story. We see the shortening of the upward thrust and reduced volume at 11631 (60), the emergence of supply on the down-waves to 11627 (62) and 11626 (119), the upthrust with weak demand on the final high at 11700 (48), the high-volume break where supply overcame demand on the sell-off to 11621 (290), and the light-volume secondary test on the two up-waves to 11628 (48)/(7). From this point, the force of the selling steadily overwhelms the buying as bonds trend lower throughout the session. Writing three-digit volume numbers within a chart grid was impractical. The next adjustment came easy: plot the volume as a histogram below the corresponding price movement.

---

[6] Wyckoff, *Wall Street Ventures and Adventures*, 176.

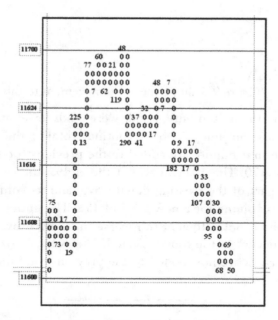

FIGURE 9.4 December 1993 Bonds Three-Tick Tape Reading Chart

Now that we know the basic ingredients for making a wave chart, let's go through the mechanics of determining the waves and their volumes and plotting them on the chart. For the $\frac{1}{32}$nd wave chart, we begin with a worksheet referred to as a "one-minute tape." It is simply a tabular listing of the closing price for each minute and its corresponding volume. As before, when no trade occurs during a time period, the slot is filled with a horizontal line. We are going to examine the price movement in September 2001 bonds on June 15, 2001. On the previous day, an up-wave peaked at 10123 shortly after 2 P.M. EST, and prices then declined to close at 10118. The total tick volume on the decline to 10118 was 160. If prices open lower on June 15, the down-wave from 10123 will be continued until there is a reversal of $\frac{3}{32}$nds or more. The "tape" of the first 11 minutes on June 15 reads as follows:

08:20 10112-10 170
08:21 12-8 178
08:22 13-11
08:23 11-12 201
08:24 12-3
08:25 12-4

08:26 13-3
08:27 13-3
08:28 13-3
<u>*08:29 10-11 228*</u>
08:30 18-7 7 (Figure 9.5 shows the price movement to this point.)

At the end of the first minute, bonds were $\frac{6}{32}$ nds lower at 10112. This is below the close on June 14, so we continue totaling the volume. The 10 ticks in the first minute are added to the previous total of 160, for a new total of 170. The 10112 price at the end of the second minute is considered part of the existing down-wave, and its volume is added to the previous volume for a new total of 178. The uptick to 10113 in the third period is not sufficient to reverse the down-wave. A new low for the wave occurs in the fourth period. The volumes from the third and fourth periods are now added to the previous total for a new sum

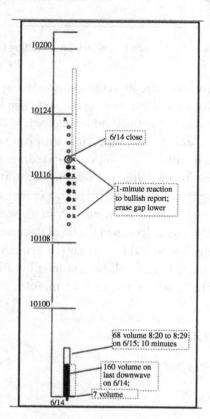

FIGURE 9.5 September 2001 Bonds Three-Tick Wave Chart

of 201. In the next five periods, bonds hold in a narrow range with combined volume of 16 ticks. If bonds close at or above 10114 in the 10th period, the uncounted 16 ticks would become part of the new up-volume. Instead, a drop to 10110 occurs in the 10th period, and the total volume increases to 228. The 08:30 period in bonds often marks the point where volatility increases because many government reports are released at this time. Something bullish was obviously announced as bonds jumped $\frac{8}{32}$nds higher to 10118. This instantly marked a change in direction and the new up-volume is 7. A line is then drawn across the 08:29 listing where the previous wave ended. As the data are being recorded, it is useful to keep a running total. Notice that no total is made for those time periods where prices did not continue lower or trade at the existing low of the wave. These blank spaces give us some sense of the market's pace. While no great significance is attached to this information, it can be useful to someone who did not observe the tape and wanted to gain some insight into how frenetic the selling or buying was at turning points within the session. The market opened on a weak note with a gap down, but there was no cascade of falling prices afterward. In real time, this sort of information becomes part of the gestalt of reading the market. Here are the next 51 readings from the one-minute tape data:

08:31 18-8 15	08:48 23-2	09:05 25-6
08:32 19-9 24	08:49 24-5	09:06 25-6
08:33 19-8 32	08:50 24-4	09:07 25-2
08:34 19-10 42	08:51 24-5	09:08 25-2
08:35 19-1 43	08:52 24-2	09:09 26-2
08:36 18-5	08:53 24-4	09:10 27-3 23
08:37 19-3 51	08:54 26-2 135	09:11 27-4 27
08:38 19-2 53	08:55 28-4 139	09:12 26-9
08:39 21-6 59	08:56 28-9 148	09:13 27-3 39
08:40 22-5 64	08:57 29-7 155	09:14 27-2 41
08:41 22-4 68	08:58 —	09:15 30-10 51
08:42 24-7 75	08:59 28-10	09:16 31-11 62
08:43 24-7 82	09:00 27-3	09:17 10200-10 72
08:44 24-10 92	09:01 26-7 20	09:18 30-8
08:45 23-5	09:02 25-11 31	09:19 30-4
08:46 25-8 105	09:03 24-5 36	09:20 29-7 19
08:47 23-6	09:04 25-3	09:21 27-12 31

(Figure 9.6 is plotted through 9:21.)

The up-wave that began in the 08:30 period spanned 28 minutes. Volume totaled 155, and the market gained $\frac{19}{32}$nds. Notice the pace of the up-move: prices moved higher or remained at the high of the wave in 19 of the 28 minutes. This is a robust up-wave. We would not have known the up-wave had ended until the 9:01 period where bonds dropped $\frac{3}{32}$nds to 10126. At that point, we would have updated our chart. The sell-off from 10129 lasts only 6 minutes. At 9:10, bonds trade at 10127. There are more trades at 10127 in the next 4 minutes. In the 11 minutes since the low at 10124, the market has gained $\frac{3}{32}$nds on volume of 41—not an overly impressive rally. But suddenly there is a buying flurry: 10 @ 30 . . . 11 @ 31 . . . 10 @ 00. Here are 31 ticks in 3 minutes (the heaviest 3 minutes' worth of volume to this point in the day) compared to the previous 41

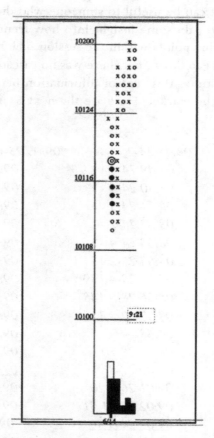

FIGURE 9.6 September 2001 Bonds Three-Tick Wave Chart 2

ticks in 11 minutes. Discussing the action at turning points, Humphrey Neill wrote: "The public is attracted by price changes, not by volume; that is to say, the public does not analyze the action of volume."[7] Three minutes later, prices fall $\frac{3}{32}$nds. We now have two up-waves on the chart. The first lasted 28 minutes and gained $\frac{19}{32}$nds on 159 volume; the second lasted 14 minutes and gained $\frac{8}{32}$nds on 72 volume—about 50 percent the effort and reward. The second up-wave exceeded the top of the first up-wave by only $\frac{3}{32}$nds. In an uptrend, when the duration, length, and volume of the buying waves begin to diminish, one should be alert to a possible change of trend. The same is possible when the duration, size, and volume of the selling waves begin to increase. (This is dramatically evident at the top on Figure 9.4.) Unfortunately, as with most tape reading observations, this is not an ironclad rule. It is best thought of as a guideline. (There are instances when the up-waves in a rising market will inch along on declining volume because of a lack of selling. It will continue until supply emerges.) The same duality that brightens/darkens every aspect of our lives also exists in interpreting markets. We left off with the second buying wave of the day ending at 10200 and the beginning of a selling wave. Although the diminished volume on the second buying wave and the shortening of the upward thrust make us wary of a possible trend change, nothing overtly bearish has occurred. Let's examine more of the tape:

09:22 10127-12 43	09:40 25-2 48	09:58 25-1
09:23 28-7	09:41 25-4 52	09:59 26-1
09:24 29-7	09:42 25-2 54	10:00 29-7 56
09:25 29-2	09:43 26-2	10:01 29-10 66
09:26 30-3 19	09:44 25-3 59	10:02 28-3
<u>09:27 30-2 21</u>	09:45 26-7	10:03 28-4
09:28 29-3	<u>09:46 24-4 70</u>	10:04 26-4 11
09:29 29-6	09:47 25-9	10:05 27-7
09:30 26-9 18	09:48 27-2 11	10:06 27-2
09:31 28-6	09:49 25-4	10:07 24-7 27
09:32 28-2	09:50 26-8	10:08 23-7 34
09:33 28-3	09:51 26-2	10:09 23-4 38
09:34 28-3	09:52 25-9	10:10 22-5 43
09:35 28-7	09:53 25-4	10:11 23-5
09:36 27-1	09:54 26-1	10:12 23-6
09:37 26-1 41	09:55 —	10:13 23-3

---

[7] Neill, p. 41.

(Figure 9.7 is plotted to this point.)

The selling wave that began from 10200 was small and lasted only 5 minutes. There is nothing bearish about this behavior. But look at the next buying wave of the day. It lasted only 5 minutes compared with previous rallies of 28 and 14 minutes. This up-move netted $\frac{3}{32}$nds on a move to a lower high and volume diminished. The buying power is tired. A bearish change in behavior occurs in the next selling wave. Here the duration and volume are greater than on any of the down-waves that originated during this session.

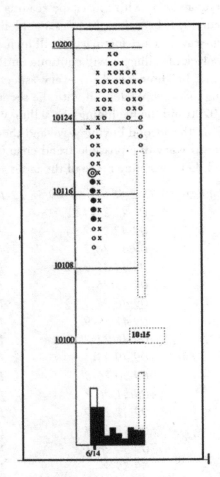

FIGURE 9.7   September 2001 Bonds Three-Tick Wave Chart 3

Two minutes after the low at 10124, a $\frac{3}{32}$nd reversal occurs. Look at the pace of the advance from 10124 to 10129. During this 15-minute buying wave, prices advance or hold the high in only three periods. Such behavior reflects weak demand and little interest in bonds. The market is now vulnerable to a larger downturn. The reversal occurs at 10:04 on the downtick to 10126. A tape reader would go short and protect above 10200. Bonds continue to slide, and we see a 10121 print on the tape at 10:15. The market has now fallen through the support at 10124 where two of the last three selling waves had held. More of the tape action is listed next:

10:16 10122-5
10:17 23-5
10:18 23-6
10:19 21-6 89 (There has been no downward progress, but volume continues to build. The volume is now heavier than on the previous selling wave.)
10:20 20-7 96
10:21 18-9 105
10:22 19-3
10:23 18-9 117
10:24 19-11
10:25 17-10 138 (Traders have placed stops below the previous day's close at 10118—a "pivot point" for some systems—as the market moves into negative territory for the session.)
10:26 18-4
10:27 18-6
10:28 16-8 156
10:29 16-9 165
10:30 15-7 172 (Humphrey Neill said the "market is honeycombed with buying and selling orders." The whole numbers and half-numbers are favorite levels where traders place orders to buy and sell. Thus, it is not surprising to see some hesitation caused by shorts taking profits and new longs buying around 10116.)
10:31 16-3
10:32 15-7 182
10:33 15-6 188
10:34 16-5
10:35 15-3 196
10:36 15-7 203
10:37 15-2 205

10:38 15-2 207
10:39 14-10 217
10:40 13-7 224
10:41 14-5
10:42 15-1
10:43 15-6

After holding for 11 minutes between 10116-10115, the decline to 10113 seemed like the beginning of more weakness. Now that the market is trading at 10115 again, one might think the decline is ending. If short, do you cover? Often, especially when we think too much, we cannot tell the difference between noise and meaning. When in doubt, don't get out—lower risk/increase comfort level by adjusting your stop.

10:44 15-1
10:45 13-6 243
10:46 09-10 253 (The $\frac{4}{32}$nd drop in this period is caused by stop-loss selling as the bond contract falls below the morning low at 10110.)
10:47 08-9 262
10:48 10-3
10:49 08-8 273
10:50 07-9 282
10:51 07-8 290
10:52 05-10 300

In the last 7 minutes, the sell-off steepened and volume increased sharply. This is either the beginning of a much larger plunge or it is a stopping point of some unknown degree that can only be determined from a view of the larger price history. From the small amount of price movement we have observed, we cannot tell if this is part of larger downtrend, a brief washout in an uptrend, or part of a broader trading range. If the average daily range in bonds is about $\frac{29}{32}$nds, a day trader might want to take profits and wait for another situation to unfold.

10:53 06-7
10:54 06-8
10:55 08-2 17

At this point, we know a selling wave ended at 10105: size = $\frac{24}{32}$nds, volume = 300 volume, and duration = 51 minutes. From experience, one would know a volume of 300 on a $\frac{3}{32}$nd wave chart is highly unusual. A 300-tick wave on an $\frac{8}{32}$nd or $\frac{16}{32}$nd wave chart would not stand out. On this chart, however, it reflects a great outpouring of supply—a major sign of weakness.

10:56 10-4 21

10:57 08-10

10:58 10-6 37

10:59 11-5 42

11:00 11-2 44

11:01 10-5

11:02 09-3

11:03 09-5

11:04 09-2

11:05 08-5 20 (The buying wave to 10111 tells us nothing, most likely some profit-taking by shorts.)

11:06 09-4

11:07 09-7

11:08 10-9

11:09 10-2

11:10 11-1 23 (No supply emerged on the selling wave to 10108.)

11:11 12-3 26

11:12 11-5

11:13 11-2

11:14 11-2

11:15 11-2

11:16 11-2

11:17 10-5

11:18 10-6

11:19 10-2

11:20 09-5 31 (Here, we know a buying wave ended at 10112. Although unimpressive, it slightly exceeded the high of the previous buying wave to 10111.)

11:21 09-8 39

11:22 08-5 44

11:23 08-6 50

11:24 08-2 52 (Figure 9.8 is plotted to here.)

11:25 09-3

11:26 09-2

11:27 —

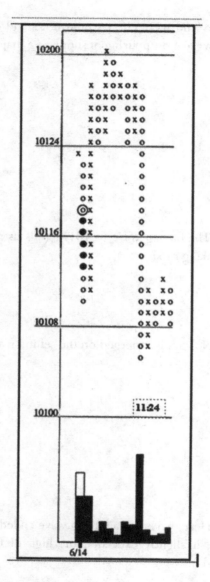

FIGURE 9.8 September 2001 Bonds Three-Tick Wave Chart 4

11:28 09-2
11:29 10-1
11:30 10-2
11:31 09-1
11:32 10-3

11:33 09-3

11:34 11-6 23 (The last selling wave retested the previous low at 10108 where support is forming.)

11:35 10-1

11:36 10-2

11:37 12-2 28

Here, the market has rallied above the high of the previous two buying waves. A correction of some degree is under way. If one is still short, one must decide whether to take profits, take partial profits, or lower stops. At what level would you expect the market to encounter resistance? Assuming Wyckoff went short at 10121, he probably would have taken profits at the climactic low or shortly after it showed a tendency to make higher highs. If he had chosen to trade the larger potential, he would protect just above the 50 percent retracement level. From our one-minute, filtered data, we have a decline from 10200 to 10105, so the 50 percent level is about 10118. The actual high and low of the decline are 10201 and 10105, making 10119 the precise 50 percent correction point. But is there any shelf of support within the decline where we might tuck our stop above? None appears on the chart but our record of the tape shows the lateral movement back and forth between 10116 and 10115 (10:28 to 10:44). It could provide resistance on any corrective rally. From our intensity of involvement with the tape, we have a mental picture of where to expect resistance.

11:38 13-3 31

11:39 14-3 35 (The market has now exceeded the previous high of the up-wave.)

11:40 13-1

11:41 13-4

11:42 13-2

11:43 13-2

11:44 14-1 44

11:45 14-2 46

11:46 13-1

11:47 13-2

11:48 —

11:49 —

11:50 14-1 50

11:51 15-3 53 (Now the market has rallied to the minor congestion between 10115 and 10116. Let's see what kind of progress it makes.)

11:52 15-4 57
11:53 14-1
11:54 13-1
11:55 14-5
11:56 —
11:57 15-3
11:58 —
11:59 15-2 69
12:00 15-2 71
12:01 14-1
12:02 —
12:03 13-1
12:04 13-4
12:05 12-3 9

A new selling wave begins with this reversal. The last buying wave gained $\frac{7}{32}$nds in 36 minutes on volume of 71 ticks. It failed to retrace 50 percent of the large decline from 10200 to 10105 and did not exceed the resistance between 10116 and 10115. So far, this up-wave looks like a typical low-volume correction in a downtrend.

12:06 —
12:07 11-1 10
12:08 12-1
12:09 11-1 12
12:10 —
12:11 12-1
12:12 13-1
12:13 14-1 3 (The 12 ticks on the brief selling wave from 10115 to 10112 reflects a lack of supply. The market should attempt to rally through 10115-10116 resistance again.)
12:14 —
12:15 15-1 4 (Here we go!!)
12:16 13-2
12:17 —
12:18 —
12:19 —
12:20 12-1 3

The market died at 10115 as volume dwindled to four ticks in 6 minutes. Within the rally from 10105, the last buying wave marked the first failure to make a higher high. With the last down-wave attracting no sellers, the market was in position to move higher. Instead, the buyers disappeared. It is not uncommon for trading to become listless at this time of day as traders in the Eastern time zone depart for lunch. Do you believe the old adage "Never sell a dull market" is correct? Figure 9.9 ended at 12:15.

12:21 12-2 5
12:22 —
12:23 13-1
12:24 13-2
12:25 —
12:26 12-1 9
12:27 11-1 10
12:28 12-1
12:29 —
12:30 —
12:31 12-2
12:32 12-2
12:33 12-2
12:34 —
12:35 —
12:36 13-1
12:37 12-1
12:38 11-1 20

The 23 minutes in this selling wave is now longer than any of the previous selling waves since the low at 10105. It is considerably greater than the duration of the previous buying wave. So far, the slow pace of the decline suggests the market is merely drifting.

12:39 —
12:40 11-4 24
12:41 12-3
12:42 11-1 28
12:43 —
12:44 12-1
12:45 —
12:46 —
12:47 13-1
12:48 —
12:49 13-2

12:50 13-2
12:51 —
12:52 12-1
12:53 11-1 36
12:54 11-2 38
12:55 10-3 41

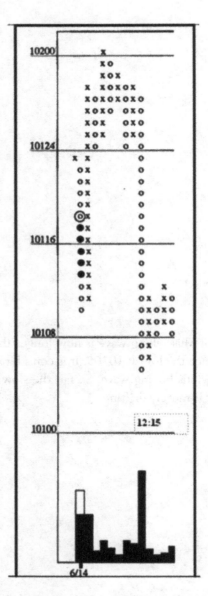

FIGURE 9.9 September 2001 Bonds Three-Tick Wave Chart 5

Since the low at 10105, all reactions have held at successively higher levels. Here is the first selling wave to make a lower low and it lasts 40 minutes. Should we compare the mere $\frac{5}{32}$nds lost on this sell-off to the $\frac{24}{32}$nds lost on the down-wave from 10129 to 10105 in 51 minutes and therefore assume the selling pressure is abating? Or is it better to judge this decline in context of only the rally from 10105? The answer is obvious: There is no connection between the two down-waves. The first is the dominant feature on the chart; the second is an indication the sellers are again gaining the upper hand after the anemic rally from 10105.

12:56 11-3 (We still do not know the immediate selling wave has ended.)
12:57 —
12:58 11-2
12:59 —
13:00 11-1
13:01 12-3
13:02 12-2
13:03 13-1 12 (Now it is certain a selling wave ended at 10110. The character of the next up-wave will be most important.)
13:04 —
13:05 13-2 14
13:06 13-4 18
13:07 —
13:08 —
13:09 —
13:10 —
13:11 — (Note all the empty minutes as trading activity slackens.)
13:12 12-1
13:13 —
13:14 12-2
13:15 —
13:16 —
13:17 —
13:18 —
13:19 —
13:20 —
13:21 14-4 25
13:22 14-2 27
13:23 14-4 31

13:24 14-4 35
13:25 14-2 37
13:26 13-1
13:27 14-3 41

The market has taken 32 minutes to rally $\frac{4}{32}$nds on the same amount of volume as the last selling wave. So far the market has failed to equal the previous high at 10115. As shown on Figure 9.10, this buying wave now has ended. You can see the nine complete waves that evolved from the 10:52 low at 10105. I should add that all of the one-minute periods where no trade occurred are omitted. A normal one-minute bar chart would leave these periods blank; a one-minute close-only chart would extend a line from the last price through these time periods leaving long, horizontal lines throughout

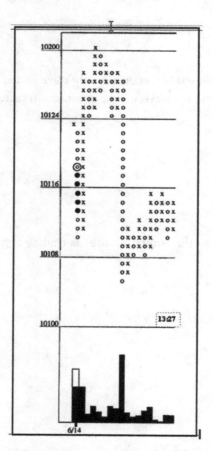

FIGURE 9.10 September 2001 Bonds Three-Tick Wave Chart 6

the chart. The last two waves spanned 40 and 32 minutes, respectively. We remarked earlier about the minor congestion area above 10115 where bonds traded between 10:28 and 10:44. After this brief period of lateral movement, the downtrend steepened and the volume increased as prices fell $\frac{10}{32}$nds to 10105. As we have seen on the bar charts, it is not unusual for corrections to test areas where trends accelerated on heavy volume. Thus the rally from 10105 has returned to the level where the sellers overwhelmed the buyers.

13:28 13-3
13:29 —
13:30 13-3
13:31 13-1
13:32 13-4
13:33 13-4
13:34 12-3
13:35 11-3 21
13:36 10-3 24
13:37 09-5 29 (The previous selling wave ended at 10110. After a weak rally to 10114, bonds are making another lower low. There is no reason to believe the recent low at 10105 won't be tested or washed out. The details appear in Figure 9.11.)
13:38 08-5 34
13:39 09-1
13:40 08-1 36
13:41 08-1 37
13:42 09-3
13:43 08-1 41
13:44 08-2 43
13:45 09-5
13:46 —
13:47 —
13:48 —
13:49 —
13:50 —
13:51 08-1 49
13:52 07-1 50
13:53 04-5 55 (The market has fallen to a new on the chart. Now we watch to see how much additional selling emerges.)

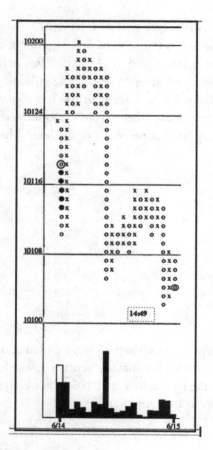

FIGURE 9.11 September 2001 Bonds Three-Tick Wave Chart 7

13:54 05-3
13:55 05-2
13:56 02-5 65
13:57 02-4 69
13:58 04-4
13:59 02-1 74
14:00 02-2 76
14:01 02-2 78
14:02 02-6 84
14:03 03-1
14:04 02-1 86 (Now we see the largest down-wave since the decline
  to 10105. It is accompanied by heavy volume. Despite the increased
  effort, the market dropped only $\frac{3}{32}$nds below the low at 10105.)

14:05 03-1
14:06 04-1
14:07 03-5
14:08 —
14:09 05-2 9 (Here it is evident a selling wave ended at 14:04. The shortening of the downward thrust may be an indication the selling pressure
   is tiring.)
14:10 04-3
14:11 05-1 13
14:12 04-1
14:13 05-3 17
14:14 04-1
14:15 04-2
14:16 —
14:17 —
14:18 05-1 21

The market has rallied to 10105, the price level where temporary support formed after the decline from 102. Following the low at 10105, the
first couple of selling waves held at 10108. Thus, it is best to pay attention to
the overhead resistance between 10105 and 10108. As we know, in a downtrend, previous support levels often act as resistance.

14:19 05-2 23
14:20 04-3
14:21 05-1 27
14:22 —
14:23 06-3 30
14:24 07-3 33
14:25 06-5
14:26 06-2
14:27 —
14:28 07-1 41
14:29 —
14:30 06-1
14:31 07-1 43
14:32 08-1 44
14:33 08-4 48
14:34 07-1
14:35 —

14:36 08-5 54
14:37 —
14:38 08-1 55
14:39 —
14:40 08-5 60
14:41 08-2 62
14:42 —
14:43 —
14:44 06-4
14:45 07-1
14:46 07-2
14:47 —
14:48 07-4
<u>*14:49 08-1 74*</u>
14:50 06-4
14:51 06-4
14:52 06-2
14:53 —
14:54 05-3 13

The $\frac{3}{32}$nd drop from 10108 signals a buying wave ended at 14:49. It was unable to break through the overhead resistance between 10105 and 10108. This also suggests the shortening of the thrust between the low at 10105 and 10102 is only temporary.

14:55 04-5 18
14:56 05-5
14:57 05-7
14:58 06-11
14:59 05-27

At the end of the pit-trading session, we left off with a selling wave in progress at 14:55 on the decline to 10104. Nothing decisive occurred in the last four minutes. We are left with a remaining volume of 50. If the market opens at 10104 or lower on the next day, these 50 ticks will be added to the volume. If the market opens at 10107 or higher on June 18, the 50 ticks will be a part of the new up-volume total. The volume of 50 will be drawn as a solid black line, and the new up-volume will be drawn in red above it. Wyckoff's wave chart of market leaders always ended with the day's close, but waves really do not respect closings. By continuing waves from one day to the next, we get a better picture of their force as depicted by the cumulative volume.

On Monday June 18, bonds opened higher but then spent most of the session moving lower. Figure 9.12 shows the 21 waves identified on June 19. They began with a selling wave on a gap lower. Starting from this point, can you identify the three waves during the June 19 session that indicated the near-term trend was turning from bearish to bullish? Remember when the selling waves begin to diminish in length and volume (duration) and the buying waves increase, the trend is reversing upward. Wave one spans $\frac{13}{32}$nds, wave three equals $\frac{8}{32}$nds and exceeds the bottom of wave one. Wave five nets only $\frac{5}{32}$nds and does not make a new low which gives us the first bullish change in behavior. Wave six adds weight to the bullish story as bonds put in the largest up-wave of the session with the heaviest up-volume. The behavior on wave nine says bonds are on the springboard as here we have the smallest wave of the session and no selling pressure. Markup begins in wave 10. A struggle for dominance occurs around the 101 line where the market

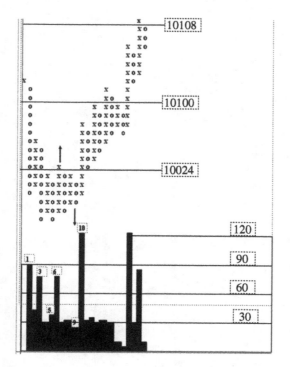

FIGURE 9.12 September 2001 Bonds Three-Tick Wave Chart 8

found initial support on June 18. The last little down-wave below 101 had a total lack of selling with no ease of downward movement to complete a beautiful upturn. I used this point-and-figure format for several years; it's always been one of my favorites. The next step in the evolution of the wave chart provided even better information and greater flexibility. It is the subject of Chapter 10.

I know a minute-by-minute reading of an entire day's price movement seems terribly tedious. But, like Wyckoff, I can testify to the value of making the effort. The process detailed in this chapter increased my chart reading skills tenfold. And I did this for years. Despite the huge volatility in today's markets and the lightning fast velocity of expectations, the behavior Wyckoff observed in 1909 provides a tremendous edge.

CHAPTER 10

Tape Reading
Part II

Another method I used for displaying the waves and wave volume simply involved the use of a close-only line chart with a volume histogram. It, too, served me well. One missing ingredient, however, was time. Whenever the duration of a wave was unusually large, I noted it on the chart. Eventually, I found someone to write a program for the wave chart. No longer were the waves plotted equidistantly. The space between the waves reflected the duration of a wave, and the width of the volume bars was also a function of time. From that point, I had all three elements necessary for tape reading: length, volume, and duration of waves. In the discussion of bonds on June 15 and 19, 2001, I made numerous references to these three elements when appropriate. The tabular listing of the data made this possible. But with the new chart it became readily apparent at a glance. It allowed me to experiment with wave charts made from any time period. Suddenly, I saw price waves that lasted many days, and the wave volume told a better story than on the hourly or daily charts. The reason is simple. Price movement does not unfold in bundles of equal time periods; it unfolds in waves. Wyckoff and early tape readers clearly understood this fact and therefore studied the alternating buying and selling waves gleaned from the stock ticker. Dissecting price movement into time periods does not impede one's view of the trend. But volume subdivided into equal chunks of time does interfere with one's ability to discern the true force of the buying and the selling. In a sense, the message of the volume is lost in time.

To illustrate the point, Figure 10.1 of the December 2012 euro contract is presented here. First, though, let me explain the chart. For intraday currency or forex trading, I prefer a sensitive tick bar chart. I also look at time-based charts, but the construction of the tick bar is not limited by a set amount of time. Thus, under volatile trading conditions, one 250-tick bar may span a few seconds, and at other times it may last 20 minutes or more. Larger tick bar charts are also useful for visualizing the broader price structure. For example, I sometimes look at the 5,000-tick bar for currencies or the Standard & Poor's (S&P) 9000 tick bar. Figure 10.1 shows a three-pip wave constructed from 250-tick bar closes on September 18, 2012. The total contract volume for each tick bar is also included. Starting from the left side of the chart, we first notice the large up-wave with 5,400 volume. This is the heaviest up-volume in about four hours. The shortening of the upward thrust on the up-move stands out clearly. It says the trend is tiring. Supply appears on the first down-wave, where the 4,100 volume is the largest to date. Compare this bearish change in behavior to wave 6 in Figure 9.12, where demand first appeared. On the subsequent up-wave, the 1,100 volume signaled weak demand and offered an excellent entry point for selling short.

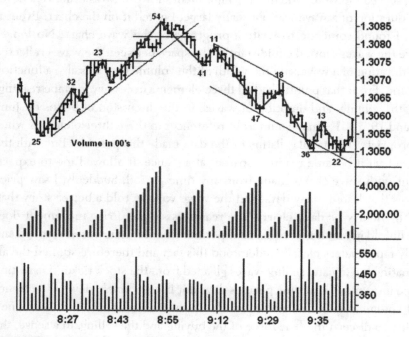

FIGURE 10.1   December 2012 Euro 250-Tick Bar Chart
Source: TradeStation.

For the most part, the tick bar volume looks like the tree line on the horizon. We can find little differentiation between the volumes, whereas the cumulative wave volume shows the peaks and troughs of trading activity. Nowhere is this more important than on the 1,100-contract pullback where the tick bar volume shows little change. Similarly, the 4, 100-contract decline from the high does not stand out as heavy volume on the tick-bar histogram. Within the decline from the high, the down-waves span 13, 19, 19, and 4 pips, respectively. The individual times per wave are 10, 16, 4, and 2 minutes. Add to this picture their diminished wave volume, and the turnaround from the 9:38 A.M. EDT low is obvious. One final observation: the next to last down-wave covered as much ground (19 pips) as its preceding wave. Yet it lasted only 4 minutes. The speed of this down-wave reflects climactic action as the trapped longs are stumbling over one another to sell out. It tells anyone who is short to start taking profits and/or jamming their buy stops to within a few ticks of the last print. Would-be buyers should move to the edge of their seat in anticipation of a short-covering rally. Twenty-two minutes after the final low, the euro traded at 1.3077.

Figure 10.2 shows a 3-minute chart of June 2011 Australian dollar. I have removed the individual 5-minute bars. The minimum wave size, or reversal, is 3 pips. The minutes per wave are plotted at the wave turning points. Now look at the rise from 1:15 P.M. EST. We see the three up-waves spanned 12, 36, and 6 minutes, respectively. Their lengths are 10, 21, and 5 pips, with volumes of 1896, 2038, and 1305 contracts. The diminished time, length, and volume on the waves reveals the market's weakening condition. They tell the tape reader to take profits on long positions. Wyckoff would advocate taking profits and immediately going short in such a position. The volume histogram is cumulative. The 27-minute down-wave consists of nine 3-minute time periods and the total volume increases evenly until the ninth period of this wave, where it bulges. This format helps one see the spurts of volume that often occur at tops and bottoms of waves. For another example, look at the volume jump in the last period of the 6-minute up-wave to the high. Within the decline from the high, all of the rallies are small and short lived. They can be used to add to a short position or to get aboard if one failed to recognize the top. The same can be said about the small, low-volume corrections during the preceding rally. Currency futures and corresponding forex markets offer a unique feature, as the 3-pip wave size can be used on each one. This allows the trader to move from one to the other in search of the best setup without having to reconfigure the wave setting.

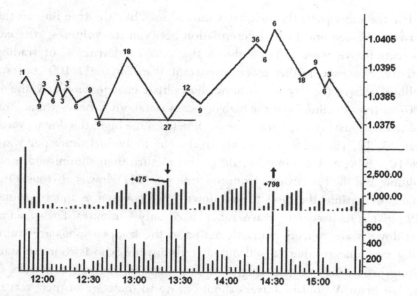

FIGURE 10.2 June 2011 Australian Dollar Three-Minute Chart
Source: TradeStation.

When trading, I often superimpose the wave chart on top of the price bars. This allows the trend lines, channels, and support/resistance lines to be drawn from the precise highs and lows. Lines drawn on a chart like the Australian dollar, where the price bars are hidden, still work well. I always like to filter as much data as possible. This way much of the intraday distraction and ambiguity is removed. Because intraday price bars can give mixed messages, their removal makes it easier to hold a position that might otherwise be closed out prematurely—an affliction suffered by many traders.

Figure 10.3 shows all the important lines on the May 2011 NY copper wave chart. It is constructed from 5-minute closes and uses a 0.0025 reversal. The minimum tick in copper is 0.0005 valued at $12.50. Thus, a 1-cent move from 4.38 to 4.39, equals $250. The chart provides a tour de force of wave analysis. Wave time and volume are plotted at the turning points. Starting from the 8:40 A.M. EST low, copper rallies over 2.5 cents in 35 minutes. Next, we see seven waves of lateral movement in which the volume diminishes. Notice the fifth wave where the market slips 1.40 cents on rounded volume of 300 contracts. The next down-wave spans 0.60 cents on volume of 200 contracts. The two waves span 5 minutes and 10 minutes, respectively. Many times a 10-minute wave will have larger volume than a 5-minute wave when they occur consecutively. The small volume and size of the latter tell us May copper is on the springboard, an ideal place to go long. The following up-wave runs 2.65 cents in 55 minutes and speaks of strong demand. No supply appears on the 10-minute reaction. The next up-wave gains another 1.25 cents in only 25 minutes, but volume falls sharply. It is the first sign of weakening demand. From this point, the action of the sellers begins to dominate the chart.

After two small waves, down and up, an overtly bearish change in behavior occurs. Copper has a shallow decline but it lasts 30 minutes, the most downtime since the 8:40 A.M. low. It is also the largest sell-off since copper lifted off the springboard. Now the market has a fast rally above the previous high. In the third 5-minute bar of this rally, the wave volume triples and prices close well off the high—a potential upthrust. The next down-wave extends slightly below the low of the previous sell-off; it is larger and spans another 30 minutes. The change in trend has become obvious. Prices now creep a mere 0.30 cents higher over the next 45 minutes underscoring the total lack of demand. (Wyckoff described this as a springboard position prior to markdown.) The low angle of advance on this last up-wave shows how much difficulty copper had on this rally. Such information was not as apparent on the tape reading charts. From the April 21 high, copper prices fell 40 cents over the next nine sessions.

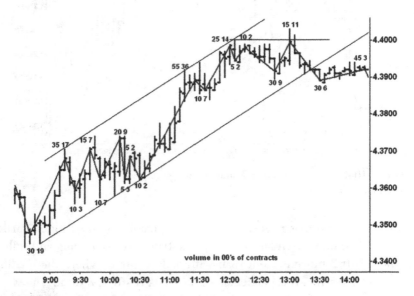

FIGURE 10.3 May 2011 Copper Wave Chart
Source: TradeStation.

Figure 10.4 presents a 0.50-point wave atop a 5-minute chart of the June 2011 S&P contract on May 6, 2011. It shows the kind of trading turn that one sees every day. For the S&P, wave volumes are noted in thousands of contracts. Here we see a resistance line at 1349.50, which is penetrated a few hours later. The volume reaches the highest level for any previous up-wave and the S&P appears at the beginning of a larger rally. Anyone who trades the S&P regularly knows to be on guard for a whipsaw whenever a new high or low is made. It's the nature of the beast. The reaction off this high draws out the heaviest volume in the last five down–waves, but it's not overt. Its modest size makes it seem less threatening. But the next up-wave speaks to us: no ease of upward movement, no demand, potential upthrust on previous up-wave, and the risk to the previous high is only 0.75 points or $37.50 per contract. You can't ask for anything better. A short can be entered as soon as the wave shows a 0.50-point reversal. Twenty-five minutes later, the S&P traded 7.25 points lower. By 2:40 P.M., it had fallen another 11 points—all this from a subtle change in behavior.

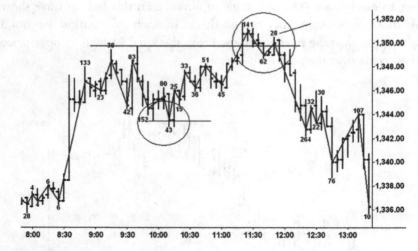

FIGURE 10.4   June 2011 S&P 5-Minute Chart
Source: TradeStation.

It's the volume that makes wave charts valuable. As mentioned earlier, time-based volume often fails to reveal the true force of buying and selling. Nowhere is this more evident than with daily volume, where the readings look about the same. It is particularly true of daily stock volume. The waves (minimum size of 10 cents) on the U.S. Steel daily chart (Figure 10.5) tell a typical story. I have included the daily volume so it can be compared with the clarity of the wave volume. The sell-off in October 2010 consists of two large down-waves with volumes of 56 and 64 million shares each. On the day before the second wave ended, the actual volume rose to 19 million, the largest on the chart. Following the low on October 27, price closed higher for seven consecutive days on total volume of 91 million shares, the heaviest up-volume since early March. Actual volume for the same period does not stand out and looks very much like the readings in early October. While the wave volume looked climactic at the October low, there was no low-volume pullback to enter a long position. But the wide-range up-bar off the low signaled the presence of demand. The high-volume liftoff indicated that the force of the buying had overcome supply. And the greatly diminished wave volumes on the three down-waves within the November correction reflected a lack of supply—especially the 19 million down-wave. Over the next 17 sessions, there are two up-waves spanning nine and seven days, respectively. Between them is a one-day correction. Strong demand enters on the two up-waves. After a shallow correction in December, the stock makes another new high on the first trading day of January 2011. Notice the low wave volume that indicates no demand. This high marked the beginning of a top formation that lasted for several months prior to a large sell-off.

See how the waves themselves act almost like moving averages. In the mark-up stage, prices may rise for 10 or more days without a correction on a closing basis. From the low of the down arrow, the stock rallied for

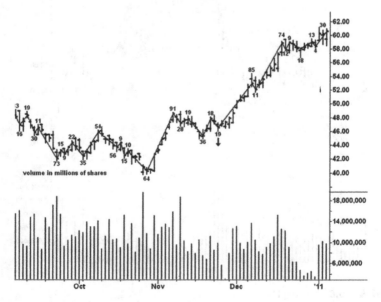

FIGURE 10.5 U.S. Steel Daily Chart
Source: TradeStation.

17 days. The one correction lasted only a day. This is a perfect example of the wave moving in an uninterrupted manner like a moving average. The one little correction was really a buying opportunity for a momentum trader.

Figure 10.6 of Boeing (10-cent wave size) typifies the most common trade one frequently encounters. When we examine the bar chart alone, we see the vertical price rise at the end of April 2011. This behavior certainly had all the earmarks of a buying climax, but the actual volume failed to signal the supply on the first down-wave. The wave volume gave a much clearer picture of supply on the first down-wave. Here the cumulative volume revealed the greatest selling pressure since mid-December 2010 and it is followed by a low-volume secondary test of the high The bearish wave volume made this trade effortless. It was aided later by the pristine line drawn across the low of the first down-wave. After the line was penetrated, two minor rallies stopped against it. On the last wave, at the bottom of the down-channel, supply dried up and the stock had a brief rally. It was unable to move above the first low made after the high. In August, Boeing found support around the 56 level.

As we have seen, Wyckoff's tape reading chart involved surveying every price change, something impractical given today's volatility. To avoid this problem, I use a wave chart based on the closing prices of any time period

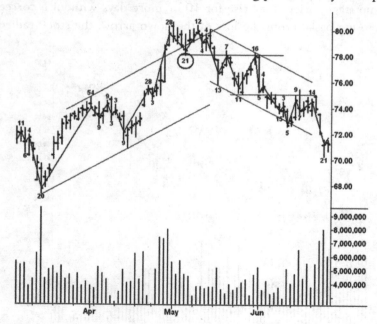

FIGURE 10.6 Boeing Daily Chart
Source: TradeStation.

from one minute to one day. Yet this is inconsistent because I am still rely-ing on time-based data. To avoid this inconsistency, I often use tick-based charts. A tick bar chart consists of individual price bars based on a predeter-mined number of ticks or price changes. For example, every 3,000-tick bar has the same number of price changes. Under normal trading conditions, a 3,000-tick bar chart of the S&P spans approximately five minutes. When trading activity increases after the release of an economic report, however, three bars of 3,000 ticks each may occur within five minutes. Thus a tick bar chart reflects trading activity. The volume plotted below the individual tick bars shows the actual numbers of shares or contracts traded. But the dura-tion of the tick bars differs. One may span 4 minutes and the next one last 18 minutes. It all depends on the speed of trading. Wyckoff saw the impor-tance of activity. He had no way to make tick bar charts. Instead, he used a cruder method for judging the activity of the stock market in general: he measured the distance the ticker tape traveled in inches per wave.

Speaking of pristine behavior, the price/volume action on the 500-tick bar chart of December 2012 gold (Figure 10.7) takes the cake. Clues abound about the coming down-wave on September 25, 2012, a day when the S&P and many stocks were also hit by heavy selling (discussed in Chapter 11). The story starts with the shortening of the upward thrust on the final up-wave to the high, where the volume (2.0k) shrinks dramatically. More overt clues are the next two down-waves on 5.9k and 5.1k, respectively. On the secondary test of the top, the wave volume increases to 4.1k. Despite this large effort, gold refuses to make a new high and we now know the market has encountered supply. On the ensuing sell-off, the down-wave volume (6.9k) is the largest on the chart to date. A relatively flat, three-wave pattern unfolds from this low. The message of the third wave is overtly bearish. It consists of 7.2k volume, spans 54 minutes, and has a very low angle of ascent. Here, we have a great deal of time and volume without making any upward progress (also on Figure 10.3), the personification of weakness. Always pay close attention when this behavior appears on a wave chart. It offers a high-probability trade setup.

Similar behavior occurred in Tennant Corp. (Figure 10.8) during January 2012. Here we have a 10-cent wave applied to daily prices. Support formed in December 2011, but the first rally off this low failed to attract enough demand to sustain itself. The retest was most disconcerting as prices hovered for days just above the low. One down-wave during this period of lateral movement lasted five days. The slow time coupled with the very heavy volume and rela-tively flat angle of decline could be interpreted as sellers absorbing all buying. The bullish interpretation says bag holding is taking place as the buyers steadily

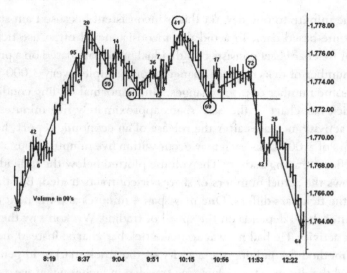

FIGURE 10.7 December '12 Gold 500-Tick Bar Chart
Source: TradeStation.

take all offers. Two up-waves later the buyers show their hand as the stock rallies on even heavier volume. On the final down-wave, the sellers manage to break through the support line but there is no downward follow through and prices rally briskly. These nearly flat waves represent compression.

One of the most common trade setups involves shortening of the thrust. Traders often confuse shortening of the thrust with springs and upthrusts.

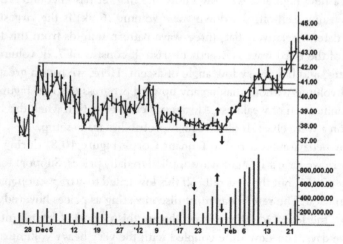

FIGURE 10.8 Tennant Corporation Daily Chart
Source: TradeStation.

The name matters little. Shortening of the thrust is diminished progress as measured from high to high or low to low. When shortening of the thrust occurs on very low volume or heavy volume the message becomes more apparent. It requires a minimum of three impulses, which may not always coincide with wave lines. Figure 10.9 of Cliffs Natural Resources demonstrates much of this behavior. If I wanted to specialize in a small handful of stocks, CLF would be one of my choices. The 10-cent wave size works well and the stock has plenty of volume and volatility. On October 13, 2011, CLF held its earlier low at 11:00 A.M. despite the increased volume (159k). This was a minor double bottom and an orderly three-wave impulse began. They are identified by drawing horizontal lines above the high points. The shortening of the upward thrust stands out clearly on the third wave where the volume (41k) was substantially lower than on the previous up-wave. From this high, the stock corrected its recent rally. The next impulse consisted of four highs with shortening of the thrust in the final wave where the up-volume (36k) was the lowest since the 11:00 A.M. low. From this high, the market traced a two-wave pattern in which the second wave experienced a spring rather than shortening of the thrust. The final rally subdivided into two up-waves but the price bars show three. I always measure shortening of the thrust from the price bars rather than the wave turning points.

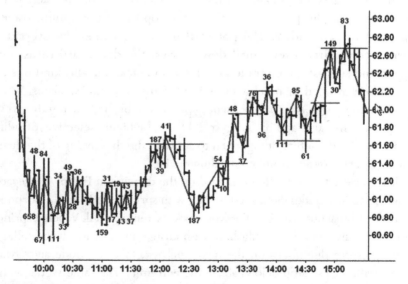

FIGURE 10.9 Cliffs Natural Resources 5-Minute Chart
Source: TradeStation.

Since shortening of the thrust stands out as the most common trade set-up on intraday charts, I have formulated a few guidelines. Do not consider them to be ironclad rules.

1. After three or four successive waves or impulses up or down, look for a shortening of the thrust in the final wave. The wave usually makes little progress and the volume declines, indicating tired demand and/or loss of momentum. Sometimes the wave volume is heavy, but the shortening of the thrust indicates the large effort produced little reward. The so-called Three-Push Method ties the same behavior to divergences on an oscillator but makes no mention of thrust shortening.
2. When there are more than four successive waves and shortening of the thrust persists, the trend may be too strong to trade against.
3. When there are only two waves with small progress in the second wave, consider a spring or upthrust. Ideally, the volume should be low; however, small progress with heavy volume is acceptable.
4. The shortening of the thrust is determined mostly by the price bars' highs and lows rather than by the waves' turning points. But the wave volume tells the story about the strength or weakness of demand and supply.

Another word about item 1 above is required. When thrust shortening appears, always consider the larger picture. This rarely involves the weekly or monthly charts, but a check of the market's position on the daily never hurts. For example, price rallies above the top of a three-month trading range and reverses down. The potential upthust becomes the overriding consideration. After a few small down-waves, the downward thrust may shorten and suggest a long trade. Any long trade taken in this kind of situation is best avoided or quickly closed out if the response weakens. When prices are moving above/below turning points established during the previous up-/down-waves and breaking trend lines, be highly selective if trading against the trend. Determining when to act with the shortening of the thrust setup is an art, not an automatic trading device.

Many wave setups are often centered on the drawing in Figure 1.1 regarding where to find trades. Setups combined with springs, upthrusts, absorption, and tests of breakouts and breakdowns work extremely well. When a spring/upthrust occurs, look for a bullish/bearish change in behavior. If the selling/buying pressure diminishes on the next pullback, take the trade and always protect with a close stop below/above the extremity. The same works with a high-volume breakout/breakdown. When these occur on heavy volume, watch the character of the pullback. Low volume at this point indicates a successful test of the breakout/breakdown and the trend should resume. Stop protection goes immediately below/above the pullback pivot. The day trader will be astounded by the number of these type trades that show themselves in every session. Two basic requirements: patience to wait for the setups to appear, and operating without any bias—don't tell the market what it will do, let it tell you.

I mentioned specializing in one particular stock or market for the purpose of intraday trading. To observe the minutiae, I often use a 100-tick bar chart. This helps one see many different setups during a trading session. Figure 10.10 shows a 100-tick bar of Newmont Mining on September 26, 2012, constructed from 10-cent reversals. The heavy volume in the first up-waves set the tone for the day as they reflected aggressive buying. We see shortening of the upward thrust on the first three impulses. The sharp drop in volume on the third impulse warns that a down-move will occur. It subdivides into three impulse waves with shortening of the thrust and diminished volume in the third wave down. As prices turn up from this low, longs should be established and stops placed under the low of the third wave. A big rush of buying hurls the stock above the early morning high. A tiny, four-minute pullback occurs before the start of the next up-wave. During the markup, we see three impulse waves, and again the upward thrust shortens. This time the volume remains large but the shortening of the thrust warns that NEM is meeting supply. The first down-wave from this high is a bearish change in behavior. Here, we have the largest down-volume since the 11:00 A.M. low, and the down-wave is the largest since prices broke out above the morning high. Together, they indicate the day's rally has ended.

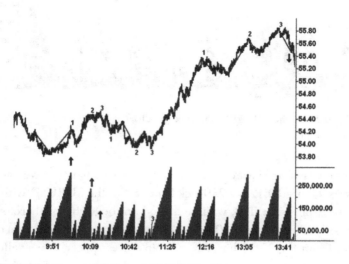

FIGURE 10.10 Newmont Mining 100-Tick Bar Chart
Source: TradeStation.

Normally when I follow a 100-tick bar chart, I scrunch the price movement as tightly as possible so the individual bars are indistinguishable. I am interested only in the form of the behavior and the structure provided by the lines. Together, they tell a very readable story. Figure 10.11 presents such a chart of the June 2012 S&P with a 0.75-point wave. It really needs little explanation. The most important behavior relates to the low volume upthrust at the high and the shortening of the downward thrust within the sell-off. The stopping volume in the down-wave to 1339.75 indicated the end was near. On the decline to the final low, the thrust shortens and the down-wave volume diminishes. Notice the very high volume on the up-wave off the low. It marked the beginning of a rally to 1356.75 over the next hour. Some might say this is trading on the head of a pin, but I think it provides a great edge for the intraday trader. Wyckoff would have loved it.

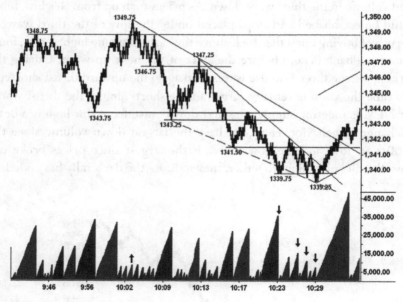

FIGURE 10.11 June 2012 S&P 100-Tick Bar Chart
Source: TradeStation.

One of my favorite chart constructions involves using two wave lines of different sizes. Figure 10.12 is a 250-tick bar chart of the EURUSD with a 7-pip wave and a 3-pip wave. Tick volume is used on forex charts; therefore, each tick bar has total volume of 250 ticks. With the wave chart, we have a cumulative total. From the 22:51 low, seven 7-pip waves appear. The smaller 3-pip wave line twists and turns along the larger wave. There are instances where

TAPE READING PART II

the two waves fit together as on the 2000 volume decline to the 22:51 low. The smaller wave provides subtle clues about market direction thus helping traders establish a lower-risk trade. On the first 3-pip up-wave off the 22:51 low, the volume exceeds all of the previous up-volumes since noon on the previous day. No supply appears on the next pullback. I would view this as a bullish change in behavior and enter a long position with a sell stop below the low. The uptrend resumes in an orderly fashion until supply appears on the 1500 down-wave and demand (1300 volume) shrinks as the thrust shortens on the final up-wave. At this point, the message is: take profits.

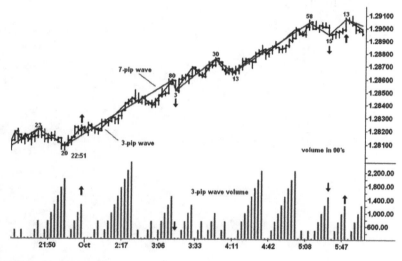

FIGURE 10.12 EURUSD 250-Tick Bar Chart
Source: TradeStation.

On September 5, 2012, I monitored the S&P 1,000-tick bar chart with a 0.50-point and 1.25-point wave plotted together. Between the high and the low, nine 1.25-point waves appeared within the three-hour decline. Arrows are placed on the 0.50-point waves and volumes where supply or weak demand indicated prices would move lower. I'm sure you can understand how the sellers gained control and pushed prices lower throughout the rest of the session.

When watching the market, I find trades rather than seek them. Jack Schwager, in his book, *New Market Wizards*, included an interview with a trader named Mr. Anonymous. This trader had made large amounts of money for his clients, but he felt they would not like his trading philosophy as expressed in the interview. He therefore had the interview reduced to two pages and refused to reveal his identity. At the end of his remarks, he made the following statement: "When you are striving, struggling, forcing a trade you are out of sync, out of harmony. The best trade requires no effort."[1] I totally agree. This is what Wyckoff meant when he described the tape reader as an automaton. Finally, the sentiment expressed in this Tibetan precept speaks volumes about a tape reader's mind-set:

> No thought, no reflection, no analysis
> No cultivation, no intention;
> Let it settle itself.

---

[1] Jack Schwager, *New Market Wizards* (New York: Harper Business, 1992), 412.

CHAPTER 11

Point-and-Figure and Renko

I n this age of algorithmic and high-frequency trading, point-and-figure charts attract little attention. They occupy a dusty, forlorn place in the library of technical analysis. The earliest works about point-and-figure charting were written by "Hoyle," an anonymous author, and Joseph Klein. Wyckoff presented point-and-figure charts in *Studies in Tape Reading* (1910). He used them extensively and most of the chapters in his original (1932) course dealt with the subject. Victor deVilliers, one of Wyckoff's early associates, published his famous book *The Point and Figure Method* in 1933. An excellent overview of point-and-figure charting can be found in H. M. Gartley's *Profits in the Stock Market* (1981 edition). Wyckoff's method of selecting stocks began by determining which stocks and groups were in the strongest position in relation to the broader trend of the market. He surveyed the point-and-figure charts of these stocks and groups to determine where the largest amount of preparation existed. In one section of his course, he wrote, "When I was doing my best work, I discarded everything but a vertical line chart of the daily average of 50 stocks, with volume, and the figure charts of about 150 leading stocks." He added, "Figure charts are more valuable than Vertical [bar] charts."

In this chapter, I discuss two of the most important aspects of point-and-figure charting:

1. How to select point-and-figure box size and reversal.
2. How to locate a line of congestion and make projections.

We have already discussed the construction of point-and-figure charts based on a 1:1 and 1:3 ratio. Figure 9.3 of December 1993 bonds typifies the 1:1 or 1-point type of chart. Figure 9.12 illustrates the 1:3 or 3-point reversal. In Figure 9.2, I demonstrated a less common 1:2 ratio chart. Wyckoff's workhorse was the 1-point chart based on dollars per share. Of course, he surveyed every price change to plot these charts. Given today's volatility, most point-and-figures are made from closing prices of various time periods. When I want to make a point-and-figure chart, I first look for areas of price tightness. My study of currency futures led me to the daily continuation chart of the British pound, where prices narrowed into a tight range between August 2012 and September 2011. A quick check of the monthly chart showed this tightness extends over to 2009. Rather than trade futures, a long position in FXB, the ETF of the British pound, seemed low risk for a tax-deferred account and would not involve rolling positions from one contract to another. The daily price rise from the 154.52 low on August 10 indicated a long position was warranted.

The next step involved deciding upon the box size and reversal unit. Let's try a 1×1 calculated from daily closes (Figure 11.1). We immediately find seven very tight columns along the 154 line projecting a rise to 161. (Note that a count for an up-move is always made from a price low; use a price high to project downward.) I like to make the count from the point where the up-move begins in earnest. Some traders I have known would immediately measure across the entire span and expect a rise to the maximum count. I prefer to break the count into phases starting with the most conservative one. One of the easiest ways to do this is to count over to a "wall" where prices accelerated upward or downward. Here, we have four phases projecting a minimum 7-point rise to 161 and a maximum 21-point rise to 175. The average of the four targets calls for a move to 168.75. A move of this magnitude would extend into the band between the 2009–2011 highs. But we still do not know where the up-move will peak. In the end, the point-and-figure projections are guidelines; however, they have an uncanny accuracy. The 11 columns counted across the 164 line called for a decline to 153, which the stock reached one-month later. Notice that prices did not trade in 4 out of the 11 columns combined to make this count. After the stock fell more than $7 from the 164 congestion line, it would have been clear a larger count should be made.

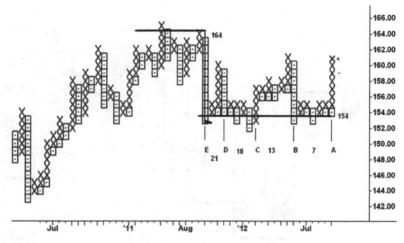

FIGURE 11.1 FXB 1 × 1 Point-and-Figure Chart
Source: TradeStation.

Next, we see a 1:3 ratio chart made with a 4-point box size and a 12-point reversal (i.e., 4 × 3); it is calculated from daily cash Standard & Poor's (S&P) prices (Figure 11.2). The congestion across the 1344 line spanned five months between February and July 2011. Its projection for a decline to 1100 exceeded the actual low by only eight points. As of this writing, all but two counts on this chart have been unfulfilled. The largest count consists of 17 columns across the 1160 line in the period between November and August 2011. When the projected points are added to the 1160 line, the target is 1484; however, another count can be made by adding the points to the low point of the count zone. This generated a less extreme 1424 target. Point-and-figure charts are noted for filtering price data and thus showing the broader framework of price movement. It is accomplished by adjusting the price reversal and data field to the point of maximum clarity like focusing a microscope. With practice, one learns how to find the right balance.

Choosing the best box size, reversal and data field for a point-and-figure requires practice. Let's take the example of Hecla Mining, a relatively low-priced stock, after the close on Friday, August 3, 2012. The weekly chart (Figure 11.3) has a tight pattern between August and January 2012. Weakness in April–May pushed prices below a support line before the upward reversal in the week ending May 25. This can be viewed as a spring. It is followed by

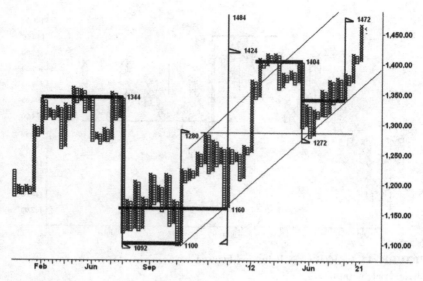

FIGURE 11.2 Cash S&P 500 4 × 3 Point-and-Figure Chart
Source: TradeStation.

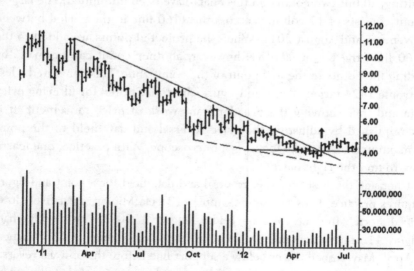

FIGURE 11.3 Hecla Mining Weekly Bar Chart
Source: TradeStation.

10 weeks of lateral movement within an 81-cent range as the stock stands on the springboard awaiting a catalyst. To make a point-and-figure chart, I prefer to begin with daily data because they tend to create tighter patterns. A 1:1 ratio chart will usually offer more lateral movement. A 25-cent box and reversal size may work but these values are about 6 percent of the stock price. A smaller percent will show more price work but only a few keystrokes are needed to change the parameters. Not unexpectedly, Figure 11.4 is unsatisfactory. First, the congestion across the 4.25 line only covers nine columns. The calculation $(9 \times 0.25) + 4.25$ projects a rise to 6.50, a respectable return; but it is not in proportion to the amount of time spent moving laterally. Secondly, the January 2012 low does not appear because the chart is constructed from daily closes and thus filters out intraday lows and highs. Thus any point-and-figure chart made from daily closes will have the same problem.

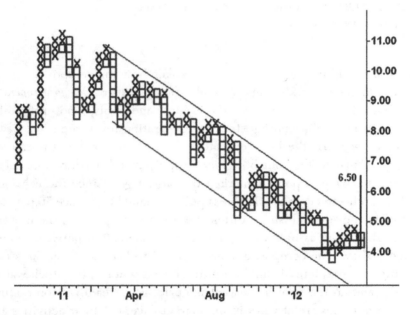

FIGURE 11.4   Hecla Mining 0.25 × 1 Point-and-Figure Chart
Source: TradeStation.

Figure 11.5 takes a different tact. It uses a smaller box size and reversal (0.05 × 3) calculated from hourly closes. Anyone familiar with point-and-figure charts would like this setup. Here, we see three separate phases that generate targets of 7.15, 8.50, and 11.20, respectively.

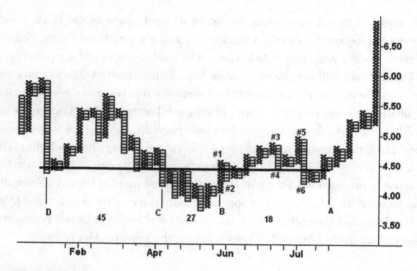

FIGURE 11.5   Hecla Mining 0.05 × 3 Point-and-Figure Chart
Source: TradeStation.

Wyckoff would look at this chart and explain how the composite operator accumulated stock during the eight-month period. *Composite operator*
was Wyckoff's generic term for the insiders and pools, who profited by
accumulating or distributing stock in preparation for a campaign trade.
Here, we see that the large operators forced prices below the trading
range in April to find out how much supply could be drawn out. The
50-cent upswing at point 1 marked the largest gain since the February
high and reflected demand. The next pullback failed to retrace 50 percent
of the up-move, a bullish condition. On the rise to point 3, the upward
thrust shortened as bids were pulled. The price action between points
4 and 6 shows the composite operator tried to keep a lid on the stock
in order to complete his line. From the low at point 6, the stock was in
strong hands as the volatility ceased and price rose steadily. I don't doubt
such large forces are at work in the marketplace, but their activities are
not the focus of my attention. The count made across the 4.45 line in
Figure 11.5 is subdivided into three phases. Count AB covers the price
movement from early August to late June. AC stretches leftward to the
breakdown on April 10, and AD incorporates all the price work to the
January 11, 2012, low. The chart is posted through September 25, 2012,
and shows the strong liftoff out of the trading range. Helca peaked on the
last up-move shown here at 6.94 just 20 cents below the count AB target.

If the stock holds above 4.45 on the next pullback, the larger counts may be fulfilled in the future.

Figure 11.6 of the March 2011 five-year note is one of my favorite examples. The minimum tick in this contract is one-quarter 32nd valued at $7.8125. The point-and-figure chart uses a one-quarter 32nd (0.0078125) box size and a reversal 2× greater (0.015625)—in other words, a 1:2 ratio. It is constructed from 3-minute closing prices. Here, the duration of each column (or wave) is plotted on the chart. You see how the early morning low at 11715.5 was penetrated on the sell-off to the final low. The first down-move covered eight ticks in 33 minutes; the second spanned six ticks in 18 minutes; the third equaled three ticks in only 9 minutes. You can see the ranges narrowing and the time lessening exactly as occurred on the wave charts. It reflects no ease of downward movement and diminishing time on the down-moves. The selling pressure is clearly spent. From this low, the market rallies 12 ticks over the next 33 minutes.

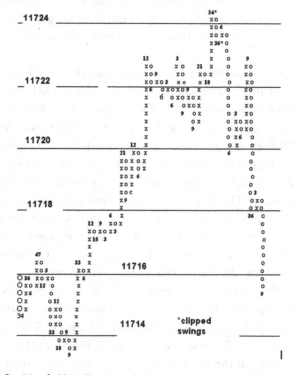

FIGURE 11.6　March 2011 Five-Year Note .25/32 ×2 Point and Figure Chart

On the way to the day's high, most of the down-waves last between 3 and 9 minutes, with the exception of two spanning 15 and 18 minutes. Both of these down-waves equal the minimal two-tick reversal, which tells another story. Prices rally vigorously over 24 minutes to the top (11724.75). Because they exceed the upper limit of this handmade chart the full swing is clipped short. This is the most amount of time on any up-wave since the contract rose from the low. It assuredly had climactic volume. The next down-move covers a relatively small amount of ground, but the 36 minutes stand out as the largest downtime. Imagine all this time spent without any ability to recover. I think Wyckoff would say the composite operator is trying to support the market in order to establish more shorts. It is an overtly bearish change in behavior and leads to the largest down-move of the day session. Notice that it lasted only 6 minutes in response to a bearish Treasury auction. The last upswing (11722.75) in the top formation lasted 9 minutes before prices plummeted over the next 36 minutes. The 19 boxes across this line project a decline to 11713.25. Prices fulfilled the conservative target of 11715.25, calculated from the day's high. As an aside, the five-year note is an excellent trading vehicle for low-capitalized and/or less experienced traders. Given the low margin rate and big volume, large traders can easily trade size to make the smaller swings more worthwhile.

It should be obvious that one can substitute time for volume. To make this information more accessible on all point-and-figure charts, a friend created a simple indicator that plotted the duration of each column as a histogram below the price work. Figure 11.7 shows this indicator on a December 2012 silver point-and-figure chart (0.01 × 3) made from one-minute closes. Supply first appears at point 1, but the next up-wave (point 2) tests the earlier high. At this point, the buyers have an opportunity to gain the upper hand. The lack of upward follow and the ease of downward movement at point 3 say the sellers are stronger. Silver then treads water over the next 50 minutes until buying emerges at point 4 where prices hold firm without a 3-cent reversal for 25 minutes. The bullish argument says the buyers are absorbing the selling. Price must continue higher. Instead, silver hesitates for 17 minutes and drifts to point 5, where the uptime is only four minutes. Because of the market's inability to rise after the action at point 4, we know it encountered supply. The down-wave at point 6 over the next 25 minutes erases the bullish story. The sellers maintain their pressure on the market at point 7 for an additional 36 minutes. Following the break below the low of point 4, an outpouring of selling takes prices lower in very little time. When measured together, all of the congestion along the 34.51 congestion line projected a decline to 33.85. Before the closing bell, December silver reached 33.92.

FIGURE 11.7 December 2012 Silver 0.01 × 3 Point-and-Figure Chart
Source: TradeStation.

Between the lows at points 3 and 7, silver traded for 3 hours and 21 minutes. The action at point 7 is particularly telling as the sellers keep the pressure on for 36 minutes. Twenty-two waves formed during this period, which is much more manageable than the corresponding 201 one-minute price bars. The capability to filter price movement is one of the benefits derived from using a point-and-figure. But I know of no way to determine the amount of time and volume for each "x" or "o" unless a chart is manually maintained, as shown in Figure 9.3. That chart did not provide the minutes for each plot. Renko charts offer this capability making it the consummate tape reading medium. I doubt Wyckoff ever saw a renko chart, but, if he had, its benefits would have attracted his utmost attention. If you look through the books and articles on renko, the same information is repeatedly stated: the Japanese invented renko about a century ago, it is composed of bricks or *renga,* it shows support and resistance levels extremely well, and it deals only with price without regard for time and volume. Fortunately, computerized renko charts do provide the volume and duration of each brick. Because of this, wave volume can be plotted below the swings on the renko charts. They come closest to re-creating Wyckoff's original tape reading charts—except he did not show the time between the waves.

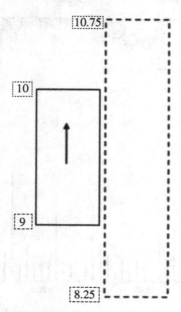

FIGURE 11.8 Renko Brick Formation Diagram

Renko charts, like point-and-figure, filter out much of the noise and ambiguities that accompany bar charts. The formation of a renko brick is depicted in Figure 11.8. Assume we are looking at a number of rising bricks with a $1 size. The last completed up-brick in the progression stopped at 10. To form another up-brick the stock will have to trade at $11; to reverse direction and complete a down-brick the stock will have to fall one dollar below the last low to $8. Before the new brick forms, prices can therefore travel within a $2.50 range. The new brick might last 50 minutes before completion. During this time, a five-minute bar chart can give mixed messages that may prompt a trader to close out a trade prematurely or totally miss the coming move. For this reason, renko charts offer peace of mind. They reduce the number of decisions. The buildup of time per brick stems from brick size and the speed of the trading. Rapid price movement causes bricks to last only seconds. Other times, a lengthy brick time may occur as prices absorb through support or resistance levels. Think of a one-point brick in the S&P between 1190 and 1191. Let's assume it's the most recent brick in an upward progression. During the next brick's formation, prices can fluctuate between 1191.75 and 1189.25—2.50 points—for as long as it takes until an 1192 or 1189 print occurs. Naturally, if the brick size is 0.50-point, the time per brick will be smaller and many more will appear; a 3-point brick will obviously span much more time. A day trader in forex or currency futures might use a 5-pip brick (-.0005), while a swing trader could use a 20-pip brick (0.002). One of the distinguishing features of renko is its freedom from time periods. As soon as price fills one brick, another begins. This makes it more akin to Wyckoff's tape reading chart, where price changes are not tied to set time periods. This also holds true for waves on renko charts.

Figure 11.9 presents a 5-pip renko chart of December 2011 Australian dollar on December 9. Here we see a double top that spanned 50 minutes. The 855-contract volume in the brick at the second peak was the largest to date. It lasted only 7 minutes. On the next up-brick, volume expands to 1,270 contracts over 21 minutes. It spent all that time without making further gains (effort versus reward). When price turns down in the next brick, we know the sellers overcame the buyers' attempts to take prices higher. Another way of looking at it is to consider that the sellers were selling at the ask price. In other words, they were not selling at the bid, but rather sold to the buyers who were paying up to own more contracts. This is the same degree of distribution Wyckoff observed on his tape reading charts. The buying effort failed to take prices higher, and it is followed by an even larger amount of selling (1979 contracts) on the next down-brick. Here a 22-minute struggle takes place. Given the lack of demand after the last up-brick, the sellers appear in the stronger position. If another down-brick unfolds, the odds greatly favor lower prices and a short position would be warranted. Buy stops should be placed just above the high of the last up-brick. In about 90 minutes the contract reached 1.0103.

Now look at Figure 11.10. I'm almost certain the stock is TVIX in early September 2011. The brick size looks like 20 cents. From the pre-session bottom, all of the lows held at a higher level. Notice the heavy down-volume and down-time in bricks 1, 3, and 6. What is the message? It is exactly the same message as we saw in Figure 11.6 where the five-year note spent

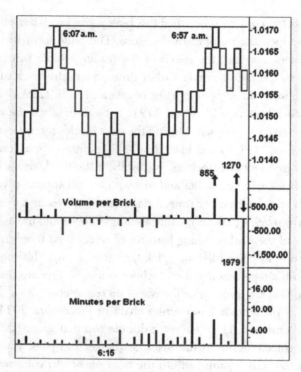

FIGURE 11.9 December 2011 Australian Dollar Renko Chart
Source: TradeStation.

15 and 18 minutes on two small two-tick pullbacks. Someone was buying. In TVIX, these three bricks underscore accumulation. Wyckoff wrote about this kind of accumulation rather than some static, preconceived model. Just imagine: at point 3 the stock spent 20 minutes as volume swelled to 200k shares and then price rallied 60 cents! At point 6, the volume was over 250k in 90 minutes, and the stock again refused to move lower. The low-volume pullback at point 7 put the stock on the springboard. There is one more dimension to this chart. From the low at point 3, nine waves can be counted to the leftmost downswing. Multiply 9 by 0.20 and add to the low (39.80), for a target of 41.60. Thus, renko charts can be used like point-and-figure charts to make price projections.

My first handmade experiments with renko charts involved plotting the swings vertically so they better resembled a point-and-figure chart. This made the lines of congestion stand out better. It wasn't long, however, before one of my students devised a renko format where the volume and time are plotted within the brick. Figure 11.11 of December 2012 S&P on September 25, 2012,

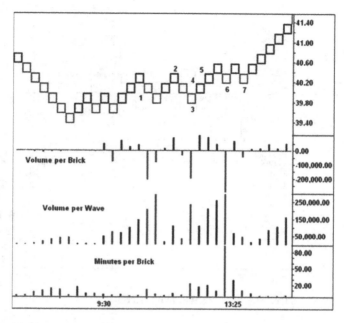

FIGURE 11.10   TVIX Renko Chart
Source: TradeStation.

consists of a 0.75-point brick size. The upper number within the brick is the volume; time is the lower number. Wave volume and duration are entered at the wave turning points. The result is a powerful tape reading chart (compare to Figures 9.1 and 9.3) with time per plot added. It goes beyond anything Wyckoff ever constructed. The top brick took 15 minutes to form, and volume increased to 35k. This large effort failed to produce further gains, thus raising the suspicion that supply had overcome demand. The next two bricks lasted 43 minutes and the volume totaled 86k; it was then obvious that the S&P met supply on the last up-wave. The first large down-wave out of this top drew out 189k contracts over the next 78 minutes, which marked the beginning of a much larger break.

I have included a 0.25 × 3 point-and-figure (Figure 11.12), which shows the entire top on September 25, 2012. The count across the 1455.25 line projected a decline to 1436.50, 1.5 points above the closing low. This chart shows the accuracy of point-and-figures constructed from small, intraday price movement. The only drawback to such a chart is the way it handles the overnight data. Because the price movement is slower at night, the minutes per column can become unusually large, and they tend to dwarf day-session data. Therefore, I adjust the scale, which in essence clips off the larger

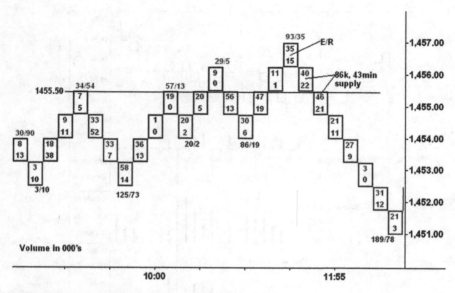

FIGURE 11.11 December 2012 S&P Renko Chart
Source: TradeStation.

readings. The result is an indicator with elegant simplicity. Here, the down-turn after the upthrust spans 35 minutes, the largest amount of downtime (read volume) since the opening of the day session. The next up-move lasted four minutes. When the S&P fell below the low of the previous down-wave (1454.50), the message was clear: **Go Short.** In *Studies in Tape Reading*, Wyckoff wrote: "[The tape reader] must be able to say: the facts are these; the resulting indications are these; therefore I will do thus and so."[1] I call it the *moment of recognition* when you sense a move is about to happen. The realization sweeps you into taking action.

The reading of the S&P 0.75-point wave chart on September 25, 2012 (Figure 11.13), gave the same insight as the message on the renko and point-and-figure charts. Look at the shortening of the upward thrust and the large effort on the last up-wave (59k). The wave volume was the heaviest on the chart up to that point, and price exceeded the previous high by only one-half point. But it's the large wave volume that drives home the message as the force of the buying encountered a larger force of supply. The sell-off below the previous low (1455), said the die was cast and immediate action warranted. In this instance, the bearish change in behavior (i.e., upthrust and large effort with no reward) was not followed by a low-volume pullback. The market fell three points on 187k volume before having a minor correction to 1452.50.

[1] Rollo Tape [pseud.], *Studies in Tape Reading* (Burlington, VT: Fraser, 1910), 16.

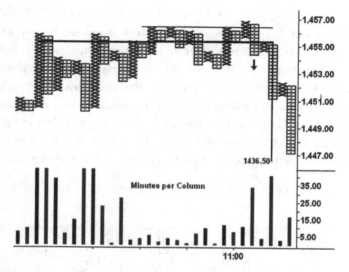

FIGURE 11.12 December 2012 S&P Point-and-Figure Chart
Source: TradeStation.

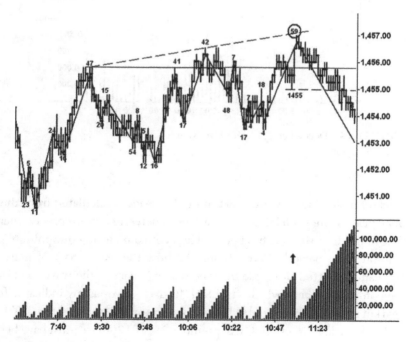

FIGURE 11.13 December 2012 S&P Wave Chart
Source: TradeStation.

For the record, Figure 11.14 shows the December 2012 S&P five-minute bar chart for the same day. I was weaned on hourly and five-minute bar charts and certainly can read the bearish story here. The upthrust/shortening of the thrust stand out clearly. On the last price bar to the high, the position of the close indicates that the market met selling. But there is no increase in volume to tell us the sellers have gained the upper hand. As I have said before, "The true force of the buying is lost in time." This is not the case in all situations, and there will be times when the five-minute chart provides a better picture of events; however, it occurs too rarely.

FIGURE 11.14   December 2012 S&P Five-Minute Chart
Source: TradeStation.

Wyckoff maintained a wave chart of market leaders calculated from their intraday price swings. Originally, it was constructed in a more precise manner but in modern times it has been calculated from closing one-minute or five-minute time periods. Wyckoff showed how the wave chart of market leaders can be plotted alongside the tape reading chart so the waves on both can be compared. The wave chart of S&P futures serves as my indicator for the market at large. I know of traders who monitor the waves in the SPY for clues about market direction. On September 25, 2012, there must have been hundreds of stocks with wave or renko charts that flashed the same bearish

POINT-AND-FIGURE AND RENKO

message as the S&P. I randomly selected a 10-cent renko chart of Union Pacific (Figure 11.15) for that date and the bearish evidence stood out at a glance. Hopefully, you see it. At the turning points on the chart, I have plotted the wave volume (in thousands) and the number of minutes. If we had to choose one brick that told us what to expect, we would have to select the 128k down-brick at 11:54 A.M. EDT. The volume in this one 10-cent brick exceeded the volume on the 60-cent up-wave, where a total of 104k shares traded. The total wave volume on the decline to the 11:54 A.M. low exceeded the volumes on the previous two up-waves combined. So this is the spot on the chart where we know what will happen. The down-move to the 11:54 A.M. low occurred about eight minutes after the decline below 1455 on the S&P wave chart. Yet UNP held for another 21 minutes before it followed the S&P lower. This lag time would have benefited anyone trading UNP.

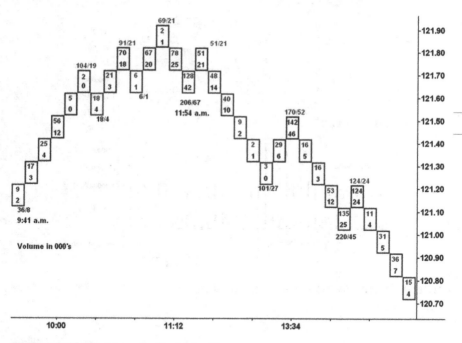

FIGURE 11.15 Union Pacific Renko Chart
Source: TradeStation.

Larger brick sizes work very well for trading the intermediate swings. For stocks trading above $20 per share, I like to use 30-cent bricks. Figure 11.16 shows 4-point bricks calculated from S&P continuation data. By filtering so much of the intraday noise, this chart makes it easier to hold trades for 20 points or more per contract. The first large up-wave spans most of three sessions on 4.74 million contract volume. One-fourth of that volume emerged in the second brick (1) of the wave and again in the final brick (2). The one served as the prime mover, and the other signaled stopping action. After this climactic action, profits should have been taken as soon as a down-brick formed. Twenty-eight points were captured between these two bricks. The wave volume on the ensuing down-move was less than recorded in the second brick of the up-wave. At (3), the S&P tried to absorb through the over-head resistance. Only one brick printed in the next down-wave (4), and it had large volume. As soon as a brick formed above the horizontal line, we would have known the high volume indicated the absorption was complete and the buyers were in control. It was the ideal spot to reestablish long positions. The S&P then rallied another 24 points before supply entered the picture.

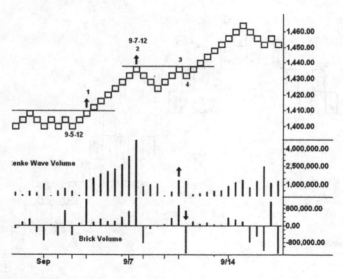

FIGURE 11.16 S&P Continuation Renko Chart
Source: TradeStation.

I mentioned earlier that my initial experiments with renko involved making a chart where the bricks unfolded vertically. The vertical format allowed more price data to appear on the chart as opposed to the traditional diagonal movement. In addition, a line of congestion on a renko chart can be used to make projections of how far prices may travel.

Figure 11.17 is a handmade chart of the March 2012 S&P on December 16, 2011. The brick size is one point. This first effort was literally scribbled onto a piece of notebook paper. The volume numbers in thousands of contracts are written at each price. Initially, I did not show the minutes per brick, but these were added later. On the down-move from the high, notice the two bricks where the volumes rose to 182k and 102k, respectively. Here, we had a combined volume of 286k over a 63-minute period as the sellers clearly gained the upper hand. Just prior to the up-move to the day's high, notice the low-volume pullback (9k) that reflected a total lack of selling pressure and offered an excellent buying opportunity. The point-and-figure congestion across the 1218.75 line, where the 9k volume appeared, projected a rise to 1223.75, one point below the high. Look at the top price, where the brick volume soared to 79k, the largest reading

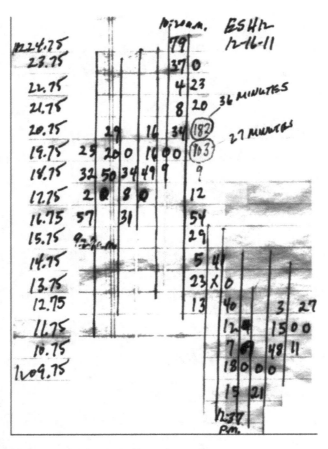

FIGURE 11.17 March 2012 S&P Chart (Scanned)

on the chart. I think you can see the usefulness of such a chart. Right now, it's a work in progress.

When I first heard of the Wyckoff method, it was spoken about in hushed tones. No one wanted to let too many people in on the best-kept trading secret. Even today, one of my friends doesn't want me to divulge all of this information. The reason is simple: it works, so why publicize it? As I said in the Introduction, I have no secrets, and I'm certain Wyckoff did not either. His avowed purpose was to help traders develop an intuitive judgment with which to read what the market says about itself rather than to "operate in a hit or miss way." In *Studies in Tape Reading*, he wrote: "Money is made in Tape Reading [chart reading] by anticipating what is coming—not by waiting till it happens and going with the crowd."[2] I'm sure he would agree with the message behind *Trades About to Happen*.

[2] Ibid., 18.

David Weis is a market analyst with over 41 years' experience. Weis served as the director of Technical Research for ContiCommodities, Inc. during the mid-1980s. Although most of his work has been tied to the futures markets, he worked for several years in a fixed-income group, where he assisted cash bond traders with timing recommendations. Weis has conducted seminars and workshops on technical trading throughout North America, Europe, and the Far East. He is the recognized authority on the trading methods of Richard Wyckoff. He is the former editor of the *Elliott Wave Commodity Letter* published by Robert Prechter and former editor/publisher of *Technical Forces*, a monthly market letter centered around price/volume analysis. In addition, he has written numerous articles on technical analysis and is the author of *Trading with the Elliott Wave Principle: A Practical Guide*. He is also one of the co-authors of *Charting the Stock Market, The Wyckoff Method*. Weis is currently consulting with institutional clients, stock traders, and futures traders. He is an active trader and has developed a unique trading tool known as the Weis Wave.

INDEX